THE
REFERENCE
SHELF

GUN CONTROL

edited by ROBERT EMMET LONG

THE REFERENCE SHELF

Volume 60 Number 6

THE H. W. WILSON COMPANY

New York   1989

THE REFERENCE SHELF

The books in this series contain reprints of articles, excerpts from books, and addresses on current issues and social trends in the United States and other countries. There are six separately bound numbers in each volume, all of which are generally published in the same calendar year. One number is a collection of recent speeches; each of the others is devoted to a single subject and gives background information and discussion from various points of view, concluding with a comprehensive bibliography. Books in the series may be purchased individually or on subscription.

Library of Congress Cataloging in Publication Data

Main entry under title:

Gun control.

    (The Reference shelf ; v. 60, no. 6)
    A collection of reprints of previously published
articles.
    Bibliography: p.
    1. Gun control—United States.   2. Firearms ownership
—United States.   3. Firearms—Law and legislation—
United States.   I. Long, Robert Emmet.   II. Series.
HV7436.G86   1989   363.3'3'0973   88-33937
ISBN 0-8242-0779-3

Printed in the United States of America

CONTENTS

PREFACE

In the 1980s international attention has been focussed on the U. S. as a gun culture, a society in which death may come suddenly and violently. The wounding of President Reagan and his press secretary James Brady and the assassination of John Lennon by mentally unstable young men who had obtained handguns easily dramatized the issue of gun control. The issue came to public attention again after an incident in which Bernhard Goetz shot four young black men he believed were about to rob him on a New York subway. The Goetz incident was one of the most highly publicized cases involving guns in modern times, receiving extensive, prolonged coverage in the media as Goetz defended himself in the courts and the public took sides for and against him. For some Goetz was an authentic American hero who fought back against victimization, while for others he represented the dangers of an armed citizenry obeying the law not of the State but of the gun.

The Bernhard Goetz case, however, is only the tip of a very large iceberg. Deaths by gunshot in the U. S. far exceed those in other western nations. In one year during the 1980s Great Britain had four handgun deaths, and Canada six, while the U. S. had approximately 10,000. Other statistics are equally dismaying: Each year in the U. S. someone is injured by a handgun every two and a half minutes; every day a child under fourteen is killed with a handgun; and $500 million is spent annually in treating people who have been shot by handguns. Yet public opinion is deeply divided about the regulation of guns. For many Americans the ownership of guns is a birthright, while for others the proliferation of guns, particularly handguns that are frequently used in crime, threatens personal safety and communal well-being. These differing groups have been locked in contention throughout the 1980s, and no resolution of the problem is likely in the near future.

This compilation examines all aspects of the gun control controversy. The first section looks at the Second Amendment to the U. S. Constitution, providing for "the right to keep and bear arms," through a series of articles by two historians who take opposing views of the intentions of the framers of the amendment. A following article reviews the interpretation of the Second

Amendment in the courts. Section Two turns to the debate between pro- and anti-gun lobbies, reprinting their statements of belief and policy. Recent federal legislation regarding guns is treated in other articles, particularly the debate in Congress over the McClure-Volkmer Bill (1986), which relaxes handgun restrictions. Transcripts of the debate on the floor of Congress are included as well as articles that clarify the provisions and meaning of the bill.

Section Three covers the arguments for and against gun control in further detail, emphasizing the conflict that has emerged between law-enforcement associations and the NRA, whose stand against gun restrictions has become increasingly militant. A final section reviews new initiatives in the courts to coerce gun manufacturers to discontinue making "Saturday night specials," and adoption of new laws regarding guns at state and local levels—a patchwork quilt reflecting the lack of a national consensus.

The editor is indebted to the authors and publishers who have given permission to reprint the materials in this compilation. Special thanks are due to Joyce Cook and the staff of the Fulton Public Library and to the staff of Penfield Library, State University of New York at Oswego.

ROBERT EMMET LONG

January 1989

I. THE SECOND AMENDMENT:
THE RIGHT TO KEEP AND BEAR ARMS

EDITOR'S INTRODUCTION

The Second Amendment to the U. S. Constitution, providing for the "right to keep and bear arms," is constantly invoked in the literature of the gun control debate. The provision seems to pro-gun groups an absolute mandate barring any restriction upon the sale, possession, and legal use of firearms. It is a rallying cry of the National Rifle Association and its affiliated organizations, who insist that their stand is consistent with the expressed intentions of the Founding Fathers in safeguarding American freedom, and that any infringement of this safeguard is a violation of the integrity of the nation itself. Anti-gun groups, however, maintain that the Second Amendment does not provide for an unrestricted possession of guns but only for the maintenance of a militia.

The first three articles in this section, all reprinted from the *Journal of American History,* debate this legal principle. In the first Robert E. Shalhope traces theories of individual vs. communal rights respecting the possession of guns to the Florentine republic and forward through British conceptions of rights to the Founding Fathers in the late eighteenth century. He concludes that the phrasing of the amendment reflects dual concerns of the colonists, both for the necessity of a militia to oppose usurpations by the federal government, and for access to arms by the citizens generally. The second article, by Lawrence Delbert Cress, challenges Shalhope's interpretation. Tracing the same background of seventeenth- and eighteenth-century republican theorists, he argues that the intention of the framers of the Constitution was to provide for access to arms on a communal rather than an individual basis, that the clause pertains only to a militia. The debate between Shalhope and Cress is continued in a third article.

As both acknowledge at the end of the article, the meaning of the Second Amendment lies not with the interpretations of historians but those of the courts. This aspect of the Second Amendment is addressed in a fourth selection by Robert Spitzer, reprinted from *America*. As Spitzer points out, the Second Amendment issue came before the Supreme Court in a series of nineteenth-century cases—U. S. v. Cruikshank (1876), Presser v. Illinois (1886), Miller v. Texas (1894)—in which it was held that the right "of bearing arms for a lawful purpose is not a right granted by the Constitution." Under this ruling, the Second Amendment is not "incorporated," that is, it does not apply to the states, which are free to regulate the circumstances under which citizens may bear arms. In this century the Supreme Court also ruled on the issue in U. S. vs. Miller (1939), affirming the right of the federal government to regulate firearms. Since then, as Spitzer notes, the Supreme Court has declined to hear further cases concerning the Second Amendment; and as it stands, however fervently gun enthusiasts may claim constitutional guarantees, the interpretation of the Second Amendment at the highest federal judicial level has decreed otherwise.

THE IDEOLOGICAL ORIGINS OF THE SECOND AMENDMENT[1]

A well regulated Militia, being necessary to the security of a free State, the right of the people to keep and bear Arms, shall not be infringed.

Since its ratification in 1791 the Second Amendment has remained in relative obscurity. Virtually ignored by the Supreme Court, the amendment has been termed "obsolete," "defunct," and an "unused provision" with no meaning for the twentieth century by scholars dealing with the Bill of Rights. And yet, many Americans consider this amendment as vital to their liberties today as did the founders nearly two hundred years ago. Their sense of urgency arises from the current debate over gun control.

Disagreements over gun legislation reveal disparate perceptions of American society that rest upon, or inspire, dissimilar in-

[1]Reprint of an article by Robert E. Shalhope, professor of history at the University of Oklahoma. Reprinted by permission from *The Journal of American History*, Vol. 69 (D. '82), pp. 599–614. Copyright © 1982 by *The Journal of American History*.

In order to delineate libertarian beliefs regarding the relationship between arms and society it is necessary to start with the Florentine tradition upon which republican thought drew so heavily. This tradition, articulated most clearly by Niccolò Machiavelli, idealized the citizen-warrior as the staunchest bulwark of a republic. For Machiavelli the most dependable protection against corruption was the economic independence of the citizen and his ability and willingness to become a warrior. From this developed a sociology of liberty that rested upon the role of arms in society: political conditions must allow the arming of all citizens; moral conditions must be such that all citizens would willingly fight for the republic; and economic conditions must provide the citizen-soldier a home and occupation outside the army. This theme, relating arms and civic virtue, runs throughout Machiavelli, and from it emerged the belief that arms and a full array of civic rights were inseparable. To deny arms to some men while allowing them to others was an intolerable denial of freedom. Machiavelli's belief that arms were essential to liberty—in order for the individual citizen to protect himself, to hunt, to defend his state against foreign invasion, to keep his rulers honest, and to maintain his republican character—provided an important foundation upon which subsequent republican writers could build.

With the passage of time the essential character of Florentine thought, which emphasized a connection between the distribution of arms within a society and the prevalence of aristocracy or republicanism, liberty or corruption, remained vital to many writers. Both Sir Walter Raleigh and Jean Bodin stressed the relationship between arms and the form of government and society that emerged within a nation. Indeed Raleigh enunciated several "sophisms" of the tyrant. Among these were: "To unarm his people of weapons, money, and all means whereby they may resist his power." The more subtle tyrant followed this rule: "To unarm his people, and store up their weapons, under pretence of keeping them safe, and having them ready when service requireth, and then to arm them with such, and as many as he shall think meet, and to commit them to such as are sure men." For his part, Bodin, philosopher of the French monarchy, emphasized the essential difference between democratic societies and monarchies regarding arms. He believed that monarchs courted disaster by arming the common people for "it is to be feared they will attempt to change the state, to have a part in the government." In a monarchy " the most usuall way to prevent sedition, is to take away the subjects armes." Where democracy was the rule the general populace could be and should be armed.

The English libertarian writers in the latter half of the seventeenth century amplified and shaped the Florentine tradition in response to changing circumstances. Marchamont Nedham declared that a republican society and government rested upon the popular possession of arms as well as on the regular election of magistrates and representatives. Convinced that free states could survive and remain virtuous only if their citizens were familiar with the use of arms, Nedham claimed that arms should not, however, be "in the hands of any, but such as had an Interest in the Publick." The idea that only freemen—responsible citizens— should bear arms soon became a standard theme among libertarians.

Of all the commonwealthmen James Harrington made the most significant contribution to English libertarian attitudes toward arms, the individual, and society. Harrington offered a crucial innovation to Machiavellian theory (perhaps *the* crucial innovation in light of later American attitudes). Accepting entirely the Machiavellian theory of the possession of arms as necessary to political personality, he grounded this basic idea upon the ownership of land. Like Machiavelli, Harrington considered the bearing of arms to be the primary means by which individuals affirmed their social power and political participation as responsible moral agents. But now landownership became the essential basis for the bearing of arms. Civic virtue came to be defined as the freeholder bearing arms in defense of his property and of his state.

Harrington's work provided an intellectual foundation for subsequent writers who linked the subject of arms to the basic themes of power and oppression which permeated libertarian thought. Andrew Fletcher's warning, "he that is armed, is always master of the purse of him that is unarmed," blended nicely with the libertarian's deep suspicion of authority. The individual's need to protect himself from vicious fellow citizens and corrupt authorities—both banes of any republican society—also became clear. To accomplish this the responsible citizen must be armed.

John Trenchard and Thomas Gordon also integrated the idea of the armed citizen with the constant struggle libertarians perceived between Power and Liberty. Their *Cato's Letters* exclaimed: "The Exercise of despotick Power is the unrelenting War of an armed Tyrant upon his unarmed Subjects: It is a War of one Side, and in it there is neither Peace nor Truce." Rulers must always be restrained. An unarmed populace merely encouraged their natural tendency toward oppression: "Men that are above all Fear, soon grow above all Shame."

Trenchard also collaborated with Walter Moyle in an attack upon standing armies which elaborated on the theme that citizens must jealously guard their liberties. Nations that remained free, warned Trenchard and Moyle, never maintained "any Souldiers in constant Pay within their Cities, or ever suffered any of their Subjects to make War their Profession." Those nations knew "that the Sword and Sovareignty always march hand in hand, and therefore they trained their own Citizens and the Territories about them perpetually in Arms, and their whole Commonwealths by this means became so many several formed Militias." Further, "a general Exercise of the best of their People in the use of Arms, was the only Bulwark of their Liberties; this was reckon'd the surest way to preserve them both at home and abroad, the People being secured thereby as well against the domestick Affronts of any of their own Citizens, as against the Foreign Invasions of ambitious and unruly Neighbours." Arms were, however, "never lodg'd in the hands of any who had not an Interest in preserving the publick Peace. . . . In those days there was no difference between the Citizen, the Souldier, and the Husbandman."

Throughout their essay Trenchard and Moyle reiterated the idea that citizens must be able to defend themselves against their rulers or they would lose their liberties and live in tyranny. "It's the misfortune of all Countries, that they sometimes lie under a unhappy necessity to defend themselves by Arms against the ambition of their Governours, and to fight for what's their own." If those in government were heedless of reason, the people "must patiently submit to [their] Bondage, or stand upon [their] own Defence; which if [they] are enabled to do, [they] shall never be put upon it, but [their] Swords may grow rusty in [their] hands; for that Nation is surest to live in Peace, that is most capable of making War; and a Man that hath a Sword by his side, shall have least occasion to make use of it."

The essays of Trenchard, Gordon, and Moyle subtly blended several distinct, yet related, ideas: opposition to standing armies, dependence upon militias, and support of the armed citizen. Thus, while the concept of the armed citizen was sometimes linked with that of the militia, libertarians just as often stressed this idea as an independent theme or joined it to other issues.

This latter tendency is evident in the writing of James Burgh, the libertarian most attractive to Americans. His *Political Disquisitions* provided a grab bag of ideas which Americans integrated into their vision of republicanism. Stressing the relationship between arms and power in a society, Burgh declared: "Those, who have the command of the arms in a country, says *Aristotle*, are masters of the state, and have it in their power to make what revolutions they please." Thus, "there is no end to observations on the difference between the measures likely to be pursued by a minister backed by a standing *army*, and those of a court awed by the fear of an *armed people*." For Burgh the very nature of society was related to whether or not its citizens had arms and were vigorous in their use. "No kingdom can be secured otherwise than by arming the people. The possession of arms is the distinction between a freeman and a slave. He, who has nothing, and who himself belongs to another, must be defended by him, whose property he is, and needs no arms. But he, who thinks he is his own master, and has what he can call his own, ought to have arms to defend himself, and what he possesses; else he lives precariously, and at discretion."

A number of significant ideas came together in Burgh's *Disquisitions*. Like all libertarians he opposed a standing army and praised the militia as the bulwark of liberty. Then, going beyond these stock ideas, he clearly articulated the idea that the very character of the people—the cornerstone and strength of a republican society—was related to the individual's ability and desire to arm and defend himself against threats to his person, his property, and his state. An integral relationship existed between the possession of arms and the spirit and character of the people. For this reason Burgh lamented the state to which English society had fallen. Having become a people interested only in luxury and commerce, Englishmen had surrendered their arms. Lauding the Scots ("bred up in hardy, active, and abstemious courses of life, they were always prepared to march") Burgh lamented that "the common people of *England*, on the other hand, having been long used to pay an army for fighting for them, had all this time forgot all the military virtues of their ancestors."

Burgh's distress over the loss of virility and virtue in English society echoed that of his fellow libertarians since Harrington. These men related the downfall of English society to an increasingly luxury-loving people who freely chose to yield their military responsibilities to a professional army. Once armies were paid for by taxes, taxes were collected by armies, and the liberties of the English were at an end. True virtue sprang from the agrarian world of self-sufficient warriors. This was gone from England and with it all opportunity for a virtuous republic. There was, however, still some hope in the libertarians' minds: America was an agrarian society of self-sufficient husbandmen trained in arms. There the lamp of liberty might still burn brightly.

Richard Price drew the clearest contrast between the perceived decadence of England and the virtuous strength of America in his *Observations on the Importance of the American Revolution.* In that pamphlet he extolled the virtues of republican America, including the prevalence of the armed citizen, which he considered an integral part of America's strength. "Free States ought to be bodies of armed *citizens*, well regulated, and well disciplined, and always ready to turn out, when properly called upon, to execute the laws, to quell riots, and to keep the peace. Such, if I am rightly informed, are the citizens of America." In his view, "The happiest state of man is the middle state between the *savage* and the *refined*, or between the wild and the luxurious state. Such is the state of society in CONNECTICUT, and in some others of the *American* provinces; where the inhabitants consist, if I am rightly informed, of an independent and hardy YEOMANRY, all nearly on a level—trained to arms,—instructed in their rights—clothed in home-spun—of simple manners—strangers to luxury—drawing plenty from the ground—and that plenty, gathered easily by the hand of industry." By contrast, "Britain, indeed, consisting as it does of *unarmed* inhabitants, and threatened as it is by ambitious and powerful neigh[b]ours, cannot hope to maintain its existence long after becoming open to invasion by losing its naval superiority."

The conviction that Americans were a virtuous republican people—particularly when contrasted with decadent European populations—became a common theme in pamphlet literature on both sides of the Atlantic. George Mason boasted that "North America is the only great nursery of freemen now left upon the face of the earth." Matthew Robinson-Morris Rokeby, too, contended that while the flame of liberty in England was little more than "the last snuff of an expiring lamp," Americans were a "new and uncorrupted people." In addition, however, Rokeby linked the libertarian belief in a dynamic relationship between arms and a free society to his observations. Arguing that monarchs purposely kept their people unarmed, Rokeby exclaimed that the American colonies were "all democratical governments, where the power is in the hands of the people and where there is not the least difficulty or jealousy about putting arms into the hands of every man in the country." Europeans should be aware of the consequences of this and not "be ignorant of the strength and the force of such a form of government and how strenuously and almost wonderfully people living under one have sometimes exerted themselves in defence of their rights and liberties and how fatally it has ended with many a man and many a state who have entered into quarrels, war and contests with them."

The vision of their nation as a virile and uncorrupted society permeated the writings of Americans during and after the Revolution. And, like Machiavelli and Harrington before them, these American writers perceived a vital relationship between vigorous republican husbandmen and the possession of arms. Under the pseudonym "A British Bostonian," the Baptist preacher John Allen warned the British what would happen if they attempted "to make the Americans subject to their *slavery*." "This bloody scene can never be excuted but at the expence of the destruction of England, and you will find, my Lord, that the Americans will not submit *to be* SLAVES, they know the use of the gun, and the military art, as well as any of his Majesty's troops at St. James's, and where his Majesty has one soldier, who art in general the refuse of the earth, America can produce fifty, free men, and all volunteers, and raise a more potent army of men in three weeks, than England can in three years." Even Charles Lee, a British military man, observed in a widely circulated pamphlet that "the Yeomanry of America . . . are accustomed from their infancy to fire arms; they are expert in the use of them:— Whereas the lower and middle people of England are, by the tyranny of certain laws almost as ignorant in the use of musket, as they are of the ancient Catepulta." The Continental Congress echoed this theme in its declaration of July 1775. "On the sword, therefore, we are compelled to rely for protection. Should victory declare in your favour, yet men trained to arms from their infancy, and animated by the love of liberty, will afford neither a cheap or easy conquest." Further, "in Britain, where the maxims of freedom were still known, but where luxury and dissipation had diminished the wonted reverence for them, the attack [of tyranny] has been carried on in a more secret and indirect manner: Corruption has been employed to undermine them. The Americans are not enervated by effeminacy, like the inhabitants of India; nor debauched by luxury, like those of Great-Britain." In writing the *Federalist Papers* James Madison drew a similar contrast. Noting "the advantage of being armed, which the Americans possess over the people of almost every other nation," he observed that in Europe "the governments are afraid to trust the people with arms." Years later Timothy Dwight testified to the strength and durability of this belief when he wrote that "to trust arms in the hands of the people at large has, in Europe, been believed . . . to be an experiment fraught only with danger. Here by a long trial it has been proved to be perfectly harmless. . . . If the government be equitable; if it be reasonable in its exactions; if proper attention be paid to the education of children in knowledge and religion, few men will be disposed to use arms, unless for their amusement, and for the defence of themselves and their country."

It was Joel Barlow, however, who most eloquently articulated the vital role of arms in American republican thought. Barlow firmly believed that one of America's greatest strengths rested in "making every citizen a soldier, and every soldier a citizen; not only *permitting* every man to arm, but *obliging* him to arm." Whereas in Europe this "would have gained little credit; or at least it would have been regarded as a mark of an uncivilized people, extremely dangerous to a well ordered society," Barlow insisted that in America "it is *because the people are civilized, that they are with safety armed.*" He exulted that it was because of "their conscious dignity, as citizens enjoying equal rights, that they wish not to invade the rights of others. The danger (where there is any) from armed citizens, is only to the *government*, not to the *society*; and as long as they have nothing to revenge in the government (which they cannot have while it is in their own hands) there are many advantages in their being accustomed to the use of arms, and no possible disadvantage." In contrast, Barlow continued, European societies employed professional soldiers "who know no other God but their king; who lose all ideas of themselves, in contemplating their officers; and who forget the duties of a man, to practice those of a soldier,—this is but half the operation: an essential part of the military system is to disarm the people, to hold all the functions of war, as well the arm that executes, as the will that declares it, equally above their reach." Then, by integrating libertarian orthodoxy with Adam Smith's more recent observation that a people who lost their martial spirit suffered "that sort of mental multilation, deformity and wretchedness which cowardice necessarily involves in it," Barlow revealed the essence of the role of arms in American republican thought: Any government that disarmed its people "palsies the hand and brutalizes the mind: an habitual disuse of physical forces totally destroys the moral; and men lose at once the power of protecting themselves, and of discerning the cause of their oppression." A man capable of defending himself with arms if necessary was prerequisite for maintaining the moral character to be a good republican. Barlow then deduced that in a democratic society with equal representation "the people will be universally armed: they will assume those weapons for security, which the art of war has invented for destruction." Only tyrannical governments disarmed their people. A republican society needed armed citizens and might remain vigorous and uncorrupted only so long as it had them.

When Madison wrote the amendments to the Constitution that formed the basis of the Bill of Rights, he did not do so within a vacuum. Instead, he composed them in an environment permeated by the emergent republican ideology and with the aid of innumerable suggestions from his countrymen. These came most commonly from the state bills of rights and the hundreds of amendments suggested by the state conventions that ratified the Constitution. These sources continually reiterated four beliefs relative to the issues eventually incorporated into the Second Amendment: the right of the individual to possess arms, the fear of a professional army, the reliance on militias controlled by the individual states, and the subordination of the military to civilian control.

The various state bills of rights dealt with these four issues in different ways. Some considered them as separate rights, others combined them. New Hampshire, for example, included four distinct articles to deal with the militia, standing armies, military subordination, and individual bearing of arms. For its part, Pennsylvania offered a single inclusive article: "That the people have a right to bear arms for the defence of themselves and the state; and as standing armies in the time of peace are dangerous to liberty, they ought not to be kept up; And that the military should be kept under strict subordination to, and governed by, the civil power." Virginia, too, presented an inclusive statement: "That a well-regulated militia, composed of the body of the people, trained to arms, is the proper, natural, and safe defence of a free State; that standing armies, in time of peace, should be avoided, as dangerous to liberty; and that in all cases the military should be under strict subordination to, and governed by, the civil power."

The amendments suggested by the various state ratifying conventions were of a similar nature. Examples include New Hampshire, which did not mention the militia but did state "that no standing Army shall be Kept up in time of peace unless with the consent of three fourths of the Members of each branch of Congress, nor shall Soldiers in Time of Peace be quartered upon private Houses without the consent of the Owners." Then in a separate amendment: "Congress shall never disarm any Citizen unless such as are or have been in Actual Rebellion." Maryland's convention offered five separate amendments dealing with these issues while Virginia's integrated them by stating: "That the people have a right to keep and bear arms; that a well regulated Militia composed of the body of the people trained to arms is the proper, natural and safe defence of a free State. That standing armies in time of peace are dangerous to liberty, and therefore ought to be avoided, as far as the circumstances and protection of the community will admit; and that in all cases the military should be under strict subordination to and governed by the Civil power." The New York convention, which offered over fifty amendments, observed: "That the People have a right to keep and bear Arms; that a well regulated Militia, including the body of the people *capable of bearing Arms*, is the proper, natural and safe defence of a free state." The minority report of the Pennsylvania convention, which became a widely publicized Antifederalist tract, was the most specific: "That the people have a right to bear arms for the defence of themselves and their own State, or the United States, or for the purpose of killing game; and no law shall be passed for disarming the people or any of them, unless for crimes committed, or real danger of public injury from individuals; and as standing armies in the time of peace are dangerous to liberty, they ought not to be kept up; and that the military shall be kept under strict subordination to and be governed by the civil power."

On the specific right of individuals to keep arms, Madison could also draw upon the observations of Samuel Adams, then governor of Massachusetts, and his close friend and confidant Thomas Jefferson. For his part, Adams offered an amendment in the Massachusetts convention that read: "And that the said Constitution be never construed to authorize Congress to infringe the just liberty of the press or the rights of conscience; or to prevent the people of the United States who are peaceable citizens from keeping their own arms; or to raise standing armies, unless when necessary for the defence of the United States, or of some one or more of them." In his initial draft of a proposed constitution for the state of Virginia Jefferson did not mention a militia but did state that no standing army should exist except in time of actual war. Then, in a separate phrase, he wrote: "No freemen shall ever be debarred the use of arms." He amended this statement in his next two drafts to read: "No freeman shall be debarred the use of arms within his own lands or tenements."

Madison and his colleagues on the select committee charged with creating a bill of rights were anxious to capture the essence of the rights demanded by so many Americans in so many different forms. To do this they eliminated many suggestions, reworded others, and consolidated as many as possible in order to come up with a reasonable number of amendments. What became the Second Amendment resulted from this last process. The committee took the two distinct, yet related rights—the individual possession of arms and the need for a militia made up of ordinary citizens—and merged them into a single amendment. As with other amendments that combined various essential rights, it was the intent of the committee neither to subordinate one right to the other nor to have one clause serve as subordinate to the other. This became obvious in the discussion of the amendment that took place on the floor of Congress.

Although brief, the discussion occasioned by the Second Amendment is instructive for its indication of congressional intent to protect two separate rights: the individual's right to possess arms and the right of the states to form their own militia. Elbridge Gerry made this clear when he attacked the phrase dealing with conscientious objectors, those "scrupulous of bearing arms," that appeared in the original amendment. Manifesting the standard libertarian distrust of government, Gerry claimed that the amendment under discussion "was intended to secure the people against the mal-administration of the Government; if we could suppose that, in all cases, the rights of the people would be attended to, the occasion for guards of this kind would be removed." However, Gerry was suspicious that the federal government might employ this phrase "to destroy the constitution itself. They can declare who are those religiously scrupulous, and prevent them from bearing arms." This would be a return to European-style governments in which those in authority systematically disarmed the populace. Thomas Scott of Pennsylvania also objected to this phrase for fear that it "would lead to the violation of another article in the constitution, which secures to the people the right of keeping arms." The entire thrust of this discussion, as well as one related to a militia bill also under consideration, was that congressmen distinguished not only between the militia and the right of the individual to possess arms but between the individual's *possession* of arms and his *bearing* of them. That is, they believed that all should have the right to possess arms but that all should not necessarily be responsible for bearing them in defense of the state. In the discussion over the militia bill, for example, one representative declared: "As far as the whole body of the people are necessary to the general defence, they ought to be armed; but the law ought not to require more than is necessary; for that would be a just cause of complaint." Another believed that "the people of America would never consent to be deprived of the privilege of carrying arms." Others even argued that those Americans who did not possess arms should have them supplied by the states. This discussion clearly indicated that the problem perceived by the representatives was how to get arms into the hands of all American males between the ages of eighteen and forty-five, not how to restrict such possession to those in militia service.

It is apparent from such discussions that Americans of the Revolutionary generation distinguished between the individual's right to *keep* arms and the need for a militia in which to *bear* them. Yet it is equally clear that more often than not they considered these rights inseparable. This raises the question of why so many Americans so often fused these rights as to make it logical to combine them in the Second Amendment. Here comments by Madison, George Washington, Dwight, and Joseph Story provide excellent insight.

In his forty-fifth number of the *Federalist Papers* Madison drew the usual contrast between the American states, where citizens were armed, and European nations, where governments feared to trust their citizens with arms. Then he observed that "it is not certain that with this aid alone [possession of arms], they would not be able to shake off their yokes. But were the people to possess the additional advantages of local governments chosen by themselves, who could collect the national will, and direct the national force; and of officers appointed out of the militia, by these governments and attached both to them and to the militia, it may be affirmed with the greatest assurance, that the throne of every tyranny in Europe would be speedily overturned, in spite of the legions which surround it." Washington, in his first substantive speech to Congress, declared: "To be prepared for war, is one of the most effectual means of preserving peace. A free people ought not only to be armed, but disciplined; to which end, a uniform and well digested plan is requisite." Writing early in the nineteenth century, Dwight celebrated the right of individuals to possess arms as the hallmark of a democratic society. Then, he concluded: "The difficulty here has been to persuade the citizens to keep arms, not to prevent them from being employed for violent purposes." This same lament coursed through the observations of Story, whose *Commentaries* summed up the relationship between armed citizens and the militia as clearly as it was ever stated. In his discussion of the Second Amendment, Story wrote:

The right of the citizens to keep and bear arms has justly been considered, as the palladium of the liberties of a republic; since it offers a strong moral check against the usurpation and arbitrary power of rulers; and will generally, even if these are successful in the first instance, enable the people to resist and triumph over them. And yet, though this truth would seem so clear, and the importance of a well regulated militia would seem so undeniable, it cannot be disguised, that among the American people there is a growing indifference to any system of militia discipline, and a strong disposition, from a sense of its burthens, to be rid of all regulations. How it is practicable to keep the people duly armed without some organization, it is difficult to see. There is certainly no small danger, that indifference may lead to disgust, and disgust to contempt; and thus gradually undermine all the protection intended by this clause of our national bill of rights.

The observations of Madison, Washington, Dwight, and Story reveal an interesting relationship between the armed citizen and the militia. These men firmly believed that the character and spirit of the republic rested on the freeman's possession of arms as well as his ability and willingness to defend himself and his society. This was the bedrock, the "palladium," of republican liberty. The militia was equally important in their minds. Militia laws insured that freemen would remain armed, and thus vigorous republican citizens. In addition the militia served as the means whereby the collective force of individually armed citizens became effective. It was this that would cause those in power to respect the liberties of the people and would eliminate the need to create professional armies, that greatest single threat to a republican society. Thus, the armed citizen and the militia existed as distinct, yet interrelated, elements within American republican thought.

With the passage of time, however, American republicanism placed an increasing emphasis upon the image of the armed citizen. Caught up within a dialectic between virtue and commerce, Americans struggled to preserve their Revolutionary commitment to escape from corruption. Following Harrington's reasoning that commerce could not corrupt so long as it did not overwhelm agrarian interests, Americans believed that in order to accommodate both virtue and commerce a republic must be as energetic in its search for land as it was in its search for commerce. A vast supply of land, to be occupied by an armed and self-directing yeomanry, might nurture an endless reservoir of virtue. If American virtue was threatened by the increase in commercial activity following the Constitution of 1787, it could revitalize itself on the frontier by means of the armed husbandman.

This belief is what gave point to Jefferson's observation that "our governments will remain virtuous for many centuries; as long as they are chiefly agricultural; and this will be as long as there shall be vacant lands in any part of America." Coupled with this, however, was Jefferson's libertarian inheritance: "What country can preserve it's liberties if their rulers are not warned from time to time that their people preserve the spirit of resistance. Let them take arms."

In the nearly two hundred years since the ratification of the Bill of Rights American society has undergone great transformations. As a consequence the number of people enjoying expanded civic rights and responsibilities, including the ownership of firearms, which Jefferson and others felt should be restricted to "freemen," has vastly increased. This has become the source of much controversy. Speaking for those alarmed by the presence of so many armed citizens, Sen. Edward Kennedy believes that "our complex society requires a rethinking of the proper role of firearms in modern America. Our forefathers used firearms as an integral part of their struggle for survival. But today firearms are not appropriate for daily life in the United States." For his part, Edward Abbey, eloquent spokesman for individualism, fears that the measures suggested by Senator Kennedy to cope with today's "complex society" may be taking America in the direction of a worldwide drift toward totalitarianism. In his mind, throughout history whenever tyrannical governments existed and where the few ruled the many, citizens have been disarmed. "The tank, the B-52, the fighter-bomber, the state-controlled police and military are the weapons of dictatorship. The rifle is the weapon of democracy." Then, "if guns are outlawed, only the government will have guns. Only the police, the secret police, the military. The hired servants of our rulers. Only the government—and a few outlaws. I intend to be among the outlaws."

Whether the armed citizen is relevant to late-twentieth-century American life is something that only the American people—through the Supreme Court, their state legislatures, and Congress—can decide. Those who advocate some measure of gun control are not without powerful arguments to advance on behalf of their position. The appalling and unforeseen destructive capability of modern weapons, the dissolving of the connection between an armed citizenry and the agrarian setting that figured so importantly in the thought of the revolutionary generation, the distinction between the right to keep arms and such measures as "registration," the general recognition of the responsibility of succeeding generations to modify the constitutional inheritance to meet new conditions—all will be serviceable in the ongoing debate. But advocates of the control of firearms should not argue that the Second Amendment did not intend for Americans of the late eighteenth century to possess arms for their own personal defense, for the defense of their states and their nation, and for the purpose of keeping their rulers sensitive to the rights of the people.

AN ARMED COMMUNITY: THE ORIGINS AND MEANING OF THE RIGHT TO BEAR ARMS[2]

Military service should be the responsibility of every citizen, advised Niccolò Machiavelli in *The Art of War*, but soldiering should be the profession of none. Freedom and military might could coexist only when military service merged with the rights and responsibilities of citizenship. Machiavelli derived his insights from the past. While Rome thrived, "there was never any soldier who made war his only occupation." Citizens bore arms in defense of the state, motivated by a commitment to the common good and officered by the nation's most respected individuals. Roman liberties succumbed to tyranny only when citizens allowed professional soldiers, unmoved by a sense of the common good, to subvert the military power of the state to their own self-interest. Hence, Machiavelli concluded, "a good man [would] not make war his only profession"; nor would a "wise prince or governor . . . allow any of his subjects or citizens to do it." A well-governed commonwealth "should take care that this art of war should be practiced in time of peace only as an exercise, and in the time of war, only out of necessity and for the acquisition of glory." Most important, the military force of society should be used only in the service of the common good: "If any citizen has another end or design in following this professsion [of war], he is not a good man; if any commonwealth acts otherwise, it is not well governed." Some 250 years later, the people of the United States incorporated the essence of the great Florentine political theorist's ideas into the language of the Second Amendment: "A well regulated Militia, being necessary to the security of a free State, the right of the people to keep and bear Arms, shall not be infringed."

Despite the militia's poor showing during the revolutionary war, few Americans could imagine a republican government without citizens trained to arms. As the armed expression of civil authority, a militia deterred foreign aggressors while it eliminat-

[2]Reprint of an article by Lawrence Delbert Cress, associate professor of history at Texas A & M University. Reprinted by permission from *The Journal of American History*, vol. 71 (Je. '84), pp. 22–42. Copyright © 1984 by *The Journal of American History*.

ed the need for a potentially oppressive standing army. It also
protected against domestic insurrection. Shays's Rebellion, the
outbreak of armed insurgency in Massachusetts, had reminded all
of the historic vulnerability of republican government to internal
discord. The danger posed by manipulating demagogues, ambitious rulers, and foreign invaders to free institutions required the
vigilance of citizen-soldiers cognizant of the common good. Thus
the Second Amendment assured "the people," through the agency of "a well regulated Militia," a role in the preservation of both
the external and the internal security of the Republic. It did not
guarantee the right of individuals, like Daniel Shays and his fol-
lowers, to closet armaments.

This view differs sharply from that offered recently by Robert E. Shalhope. He contends that the Second Amendment guaranteed individuals the right "to possess arms for their own
personal defense." Shalhope concedes that the militia contributed to the political thinking that produced the amendment. Nevertheless, he argues that "Americans of the Revolutionary
generation distinguished between the individual's right to *keep*
arms and the need for a militia in which to *bear* them." Rather
than a simple statement of the militia's place in the constitutional
order, as proponents of gun control have contended, the amendment merged "two distinct, yet related rights—the individual
possession of arms and the need for a militia made up of ordinary
citizens." The militia may have lost its significance for modern
Americans, but, concludes Shalhope, its demise has not eroded
the individual's constitutional right to arms.

Shalhope's essay attempts to resolve differences between opponents and proponents of gun control over the historical meaning of the Second Amendment—differences he credits correctly
to a failure "to understand the origins of the amendment within
the perspective of the late eighteenth, rather than that of the late
twentieth, century." Nevertheless, his effort to explain the aims
of the amendment's authors is itself marred by anachronisms.
Most important, he fails to place citizenship, especially the idea
of citizens in arms, in a context compatible with the republican
theory of revolutionary America. In the eighteenth century, citizenship, which was defined in part by militia service, connoted
civic virtue, a commitment to the greater public good, not an insistence on individual prerogative. Moreover, an armed citizenry
by no means implied an armed population. A well-regulated mili-

tia drawn from a community's propertied yeomen and led by its most prominent citizens preserved liberty; armed individuals threatened it. Shalhope misses much, even ignoring the implications of evidence he cites himself. This essay will show that seventeenth- and eighteenth-century republican theorists understood access to arms to be a communal, rather than an individual, right.

Between the publication of Machiavelli's works in the early sixteenth century and the official addition of the Second Amendment to the Constitution on March 1, 1792, stands a corpus of political theory, constitutional law, and legislative enactments that underscores the lingering influence of the classical republican notion that arms had an acceptable function in society only in the service of the common good. Since the mid-seventeenth century, English political theorists—themselves drawing on the insights of Machiavelli—had linked the militia to the maintenance of a balanced, stable, and free constitution. James Harrington, whose *Commonwealth of Oceana* was widely read by Americans of the revolutionary generation, associated political stability with the armed, enfranchised, and propertied citizen. Land gave the individual economic independence and ultimately the leisure to serve the common good through the franchise and through membership in the militia. The citizen bore arms not to deter personal assault or to protect the limits of his freehold; for Harrington, bearing arms, like voting, symbolized the political independence that allowed for and ensured a commitment to civic virtue. The citizen militia, then, was not only an agent of national defense but also a deterrent to the ambitious nature of centralized political power.

Advocates of political liberty writing during the tumultuous years before and after the Glorious Revolution of 1688 also emphasized the militia's importance as a guarantor of constitutional stability. Algernon Sidney warned of the rise of tyranny whenever the militia was allowed to decay. John Trenchard, later well known in the colonies as the coauthor with Thomas Gordon of *Cato's Letters*, began his career as a pamphleteer by chiding Parliament for providing William III with a standing army after the Treaty of Ryswick in 1697. Standing armies, he wrote, were the agents of political intrigue and corruption. Only a militia could be counted on to protect both the territory and the liberties of a free people.

Sidney, Trenchard, and a host of other radical Whig essayists shared with Harrington the idea that arms were "the only true badges of liberty." In "a popular or mixed Government," wrote Sidney, "the body of the People is the publick defence, and every man is arm'd and disciplin'd." No nation was secure except by relying on the military strength of its own people. Nevertheless, freedom did not depend on the armed individual. Arms guaranteed liberty only through the organization and discipline provided by the militia. More precisely, liberty was preserved "by making the Militia to consist of the same Persons as have the Property." As had Harrington, radical Whigs believed that property assured the independence of mind and action that allowed the militia to serve the common good. Calls for militia reform circulating during the first decade of William II's reign underscore the limits within which the right to bear arms was understood. Not the armed individual, but "A good militia," contended Andrew Fletcher, "is the chief part of the constitution of any free government." A rank and file well trained in the military arts and led by "persons of quality or education" will "always preserve the publick liberty." Such a military force had proven formidable in ancient times. Founding Britain's defenses on a mandatory system of militia encampments promised an opportunity to inspire a commitment to the common good and to train the citizenry at arms: "Such a [militia] camp," thought Fletcher, "would be as great a school of virtue as of military discipline."

John Toland, the individual most responsible for the republication of Harrington's writings at the end of the seventeenth century, joined his friend Fletcher in drafting a militia-reform scheme intended to place arms "in the hands of sober, industrious, and understanding Freemen." "By Freemen," wrote Toland, "I understand Men of Property, or Persons that are able to live of themselves." Such men, through their awareness of and commitment to the "Publick Good," had made the armies of the Roman republic invincible. Men of lesser means lacked the leisure with which "to design the Good of the Commonwealth" and were thus unreliable defenders of the public interest. Trenchard was equally committed to building a militia structure that would bring young nobles and gentry into the field, thus providing Britain with the "best disciplin'd Troops and most excellent Souldiers in the World." In the ancient republics, "arms never lodged in the Hands of any who had not an Interest in preserving the publick

Peace." To the contrary, "a general Exercise of the best of their People in the use of Arms, was the only Bulwark of their Liberties; . . . the People being secured thereby as well against the Domestick Affronts of any of their own Citizens, as against the Foreign Invasions of ambitious and unruly Neighbours." In sum, the "Sword and Soveraignty always march[ed] hand in hand." The self-interested armed individual, like universal manhood suffrage, had no place in the neo-Harringtonian thought of the radical Whigs. "Most Men do as much Mischief as lay in their Power," reminded Trenchard; it was best to "take away all Weapons by which they may do either themselves or others an Injury."

Trenchard's counsel would have surprised none of his contemporaries involved in the events surrounding the Glorious Revolution. James II's use of a standing army to enforce absolute rule had contributed directly to his inglorious exile to France. He had also advanced the cause of Catholicism in England by increasing the number of Catholic officers to the exclusion of Protestants—a violation of the 1673 Test Act—and by importing Irish Catholics to fill the army's expanded ranks. As the Bill of Rights phrased it, he "did endeavour to subvert and entirpate the Protestant religion and the laws and liberties of this kingdom." He was charged in particular with "raising and keeping a standing army . . . without consent of parliament" and with "causing several good subjects being Protestants to be disarmed, at the same time when papists were both armed and employed." To correct the situation, the Bill of Rights prohibited the English monarchy from raising an army during peacetime without Parliament's consent. It also guaranteed—in language that speaks to the limited dimensions of the right to bear arms in English constitutional law—"that the subjects which are Protestants may have arms for their defence suitable to their conditions, and as allowed by law."

In other words, the Bill of Rights laid down the right of a class of citizens, Protestants, to take part in the military affairs of the realm. Nowhere was an individual's right to arm in self-defense guaranteed. Protestants "may have arms for their defence," declared the revolutionary settlement, but then only as is "suitable to their conditions and as allowed by law." Those of unsuitable condition (a statute passed during the reign of Charles II disarmed anyone owning lands with an annual value of less than £100, other than the son or heir of an esquire or person of higher social rank) were not to be armed. Parliament also retained the prerogative to restrict future access to arms "by law." In sum, had Protestants not been "disarmed at the same time when papists were . . . armed," bearing arms might not have been a topic addressed by the revolutionary settlement. Guaranteeing access to arms for Protestants, which was linked in the same sentence to the prohibition against standing armies, was intended to ensure a stable government free from the disruptions caused by Catholic Jacobites and the ambitious intrigues of future monarchs. The Bill of Rights gave to Parliament the responsibility to guarantee the external and domestic security of the realm. That meant guaranteeing a place for Protestants in the military affairs of the kingdom, at least so long as that fitted the larger goal of maintaining a free and stable constitutional structure.

After the Glorious Revolution, most political commentators in Britain lost interest in the militia as a guarantor of political freedom. Believing that the Bill of Rights had secured for Parliament the means to prevent royal misuse of the nation's military forces, men such as Daniel Defoe, John Somers, and others embraced the argument that standing armies financed by Parliament were militarily superior to the militia as well as compatible with traditional English liberties. Nevertheless, Opposition writers continued to insist that only an organized and disciplined militia composed of the landed citizenry could prevent Britain from succumbing to the same corrupting forces that had destroyed liberty in ancient Rome. Trenchard and Gordon's *Cato's Letters*, frequently reprinted in the American colonies, and the writings of Francis Hutcheson at the University of Glasgow ensured that Americans remained exposed to the neoclassical republicanism of radical Whig theory.

James Burgh's *Political Disquisitions* (1774-1775), copies of which were owned by a host of prominent American leaders, provided a convenient summary of Opposition views on the relationship between the militia and the preservation of political liberty. Borrowing extensively from promilitia tracts written during the reign of William III, Burgh attacked standing armies as anathema to freedom while holding up the citizen-soldier as its only guarantor. But not just anyone should have access to the arms militia membership implied. "Men of property," Burgh insisted, "must be our only resource. . . . A militia consisting of any others than the men of *property* in a country, is no militia; but a mungrel army." The importance of placing arms only in the hands of those "whose interest is involved in that of their country" was historically undeniable. Rome succumbed to tyranny when landed citizens shed their responsibility for the republic's defense. On the other hand, liberty survived in Switzerland because arms and citizenship remained inseparable. The lessons of history were clear: "If the militia be not upon a right foot"—that is, if classical notions of the citizen in arms were violated—"the liberty of the people must perish."

Burgh thought that circumstances in England and the American colonies on the eve of the American Revolution justified the position held by Opposition writers since Trenchard in 1697 wrote *An Argument, Shewing, that a Standing Army Is Inconsistent with a Free Government, and Absolutely Destructive to the Constitution of the English Monarchy.* "Our times prove Mr. Trenchard a true prophet," declared the dissident essayist. Americans concerned about the constitutional foundations of liberty in the colonies agreed. In *A Summary View of the Rights of British America,* Thomas Jefferson, indicting George III for sending "among us large bodies of armed forces, not made up of the people here, nor raised by the authority of our laws," reflected an American awareness of the relationship between liberty and military power. The occupation of Boston by British soldiers in 1768 and again in 1774, to say nothing of the Boston Massacre, left little doubt that hired soldiers could be agents of political oppression. Important, too, was the colonial militia. In the winter and spring of 1774–1775, colonists gathered at county assemblies and provincial conventions roundly to condemn standing armies while resolving—in language that foreshadowed the Second Amendment—"that a well-regulated Militia, composed of the gentlemen, freeholders, and other freemen, is the natural strength and only stable security of a free Government." At the same time, the Continental Congress urged provincial assemblies to "disarm all such as will not associate to defend the American right by arms."

Such declarations merely summarized sentiment long extant in the colonies. During the Seven Years War, Thomas Pownall reminded the officers and men of the Massachusetts militia that "free government" depended on the willingness of "every freeman and every freeholder" to be a soldier. "Let therefore every man, that, appealing to his own heart, feels the least spark of virtue or freedom there, think that it is an honour which he owes himself, and a duty which he owes his country, to bear arms."

Pownall did not have in mind the isolated individual standing guard over his person and property. The citizen-soldier defended life and liberty by "bear[ing] arms in the bands of his country." Sermon and pamphlet literature published in the colonies after 1768 emphasized the same point. "A well-disciplined militia is the beauty, and under God, the security of a country," declared Samuel Stillman in 1770, using language that would appear again and again as relations with the British Empire worsened. The best civil constitution would be meaningless if the people were unable to deter ambitious tyrants by force of arms. "The true strength and safety of every commonwealth or limited monarchy," proclaimed James Lovell on the first anniversary of the Boston Massacre, "is the bravery of its freeholders, its militia."

Lovell's association of freehold status with militia membership was not coincidental. A sound militia structure ensured a citizenry ably drilled in arms, but it also defined the limits of the body politic. "The sword should never be in the hands of any, but those who have an interest in the safety of the community," declared Josiah Quincy in his widely read attack on the Boston Port Bill. Landless wanderers might be pressed into military service in an emergency, but the defense of liberty depended on a "well disciplined militia, composed of men of fortunes, of education, and virtues, . . . excited to the most vigorous action, by motives infinitely superior to the expectation of spoils." The protection of family, property, and constitutional liberties motivated these individuals to serve the common good. Hence they could be relied on to return to the "enjoyment of freedom and good order" when the danger passed. Furthermore, regular training in arms had "a natural Tendency to introduce and establish good Order, and a just Subordination among the different Classes of People in the Community." As had Machiavelli, Harrington, and the radical Whigs, Americans saw the militia as an expression of the corporate unity of society. Men of rank and substance commanded the "well regulated" militia; men of lesser means filled its rank and file. In short, the parade field reinforced the deferential social and political relationships that ensured order and a respect for authority throughout society.

Americans, of course, looked to the militia to protect their liberties after Great Britain returned Redcoats to American soil in the early summer of 1774. They also turned to it as new constitutions were created to replace crumbling royal authority in the late spring of 1776. Virginia's Declaration of Rights—adopted on June 12, 1776, nearly a month before the American colonies officially announced their independence—set the pattern. Article 13, drafted by George Mason and approved by a committee that included James Madison, declared "That a well-regulated Militia, composed of the body of the people, trained to arms, is the proper, natural, and safe defence of a free State." Two months later, Pennsylvania declared that "the people have a right to bear arms for the defence of themselves and the state." The language was slightly different, but the meaning was the same. Only the citizenry, trained, armed, and organized in the militia, could be depended on to preserve republican liberties for "themselves" and to ensure the constitutional stability of "the state." Both documents linked the citizen's responsibility for the defense of the state to the threat of standing armies: standing armies were "dangerous to liberty" and must be kept "under strict subordination" to the civil government.

Delaware, Maryland, and North Carolina adopted similar declarations during the first year of independence. Delaware and Maryland borrowed language from Virginia's Article 13; North Carolina, following Pennsylvania's lead, declared that "the people have a right to bear arms, for the defence of the State." Vermont, though not to become a state until 1792, quoted verbatim Pennsylvania's Article 13 in its 1777 Declaration of Rights. In the same year New York incorporated into its constitution an equally clear reminder of a militia's relationship to the success of republican government. Announcing it to be "the duty of every man who enjoys the protection of society to be prepared and willing to defend it," New Yorkers proclaimed that the "militia . . . at all times . . . shall be armed and disciplined." Several other states took a similar approach. Only Massachusetts and New Hampshire joined Virginia, Pennsylvania, Delaware, Maryland, and North Carolina in adopting a separate declaration of rights.

John Adams, who was as important to the Massachusetts Declaration of Rights as Mason was to Virginia's, borrowed the style of the Quaker State's declaration when he drafted the Declaration of Rights that stood for ratification with the 1780 constitution. "The people," he wrote, "have a right to keep and to bear arms for the common defence." By "the people," John Adams meant the militia. "The public sword, without a hand to hold it, is but cold iron," he noted some years later, and "the hand which

holds this sword is the militia of the nation." New Hampshire's
1783 Bill of Rights made the same point, declaring that "A well
regulated militia is the proper, natural, and sure defence of a
state." Both documents condemned standing armies and pro-
nounced the subordination of military to civil authority, in the
process underscoring the citizen militia's collective role as the
protector of personal liberty and constitutional stability against
ambitious tyrants and uncontrolled mobs.

Whether it was Massachusetts' declaration that citizens had
the right "to bear arms for the common defence" or Virginia's af-
firmation that the militia was "the proper, natural, and safe defence of a free State," the point was the same. Republicanism
depended on the existence of a sound militia. Only a strong, pop-
ularly based militia could protect liberty against domestic turmoil
and tyrannical intrigue.

The language of constitutional provisions protecting conscientious objectors from military service underscores the fact that
for eighteenth-century Americans "to bear arms" meant militia
service. Such guarantees took the form of limitations on the individual's militia obligation. Pennsylvania provided that no "man
who is conscientiously scrupulous of bearing arms" could be
"compelled" to serve in the militia, though an individual was still
required to meet his obligation for the state's defense by paying
an "equivalent." Delaware and Vermont adopted similar language. New York's constitution limited such exemptions only to
Quakers, who "from scruples of conscience, may be averse to the
bearing of arms." It, too, required conscientious objectors to "pay
to the State such sums of money, in lieu of their personal service."
New Hampshire's Bill of Rights was both more broadly conceived
and more direct: "No person who is conscientiously scrupulous
about the lawfulness of bearing arms, shall be compeled thereto,
provided he will pay an equivalent."

State after state guaranteed the sovereign citizenry, described
collectively as "the people" or "the militia," a role in the common
defense. On the other hand, the expression "man" or "person" is
used to describe individual rights such as freedom of conscience.
New Hampshire's Bill of Rights, the last written during the Confederation period and as such a compendium of previous thinking
on the matter, provides a case in point. It declared the importance of "a well regulated militia [to the] defence of a state" while
it exempted from service any "person . . . conscientiously scru-

pulous about the lawfulness of bearing arms." In other words, the individual right of conscience was asserted against the collective responsibility of the citizenry for the common defense. There could be no other logical reason for an exemption from "bearing arms" unless it applied to doing service in the militia. Indeed, the state assessed "equivalents" so that someone else could be hired to "bear arms" in the conscientious objector's place.

The same issues that informed the states' declarations of rights—the importance of the militia to republican government, the threat of standing armies, the free exercise of conscience in matters of militia service, the subordination of military to civil authority—carried over into the debate over the new federal Constitution. Federalists and Antifederalists alike agreed that the citizenry trained in arms was the only sure guarantor of liberty. Americans, unlike peoples living under arbitrary governments, were "required by Law" to train with the militia, noted an anonymous essayist in the midst of the stuggle over ratification. "This is a circumstance which encreases the power and consequence of the people; and enables them to defend their rights and privileges against every invader." Antifederalists, however, were convinced that the power granted the national government threatened the militia's place in the Republic's constitutional structure. "My great objection to this government," Patrick Henry announced to Virginia's ratification convention, "is, that it does not leave us the means of defending our rights." "Have we the means of resisting disciplined armies," he continued, "when our only defence, the militia, is put into the hands of Congress?" The author of *Letters from a Federalist Farmer* also feared Congress's power to organize and to train the militia. A select militia of "one fifth or one eighth part of the men capable of bearing arms, . . . and those the young and ardent part of the community, possessed of but little or no property," could be formed while propertied citizens were organized in a fashion "render[ing] them of no importance." "The former," he argued, "will answer all the purposes of [a standing] army, while the latter will be defenceless."

Luther Martin, the outspoken Marylander who had left the Philadelphia Constitutional Convention in protest, also registered concern about the new government's military prerogatives. "Instead of *guarding against a standing army*, . . . which has so *often* and so *successfully* been used for the *subversion* of freedom," the Constitution gave "it an *express* and *constitutional sanction*." Congress's access to the states' militias troubled him too. Its authority over the militia, he warned, could be used "even [to] disarm" it. Worse, the militia might be abused—needlessly mobilized for service in the far reaches of the Union—so that the people would be glad to see a standing army raised in its place. "When a government wishes to deprive their citizens of freedom," he noted, "it generally makes use of a standing army . . . and leaves the militia in a situation as comtemptible as possible, lest they might oppose its arbitrary designs." Pennsylvania's vocal Antifederalist minority expressed similar fears, demanding for the states the power to organize, arm, and discipline the militia as well as the power to veto a congressional call for service outside a state's borders.

Mason's efforts to amend the Constitution provide a convenient summary of the sentiments that led ultimately to the Second Amendment. During the last days of the Philadelphia Constitutional Convention, Mason, having failed to secure a separate bill of rights, sought an explicit statement of the militia's place in the new government. He urged that the congressional power to arm, to organize, and to discipline the militia be prefaced by a clause identifying that prerogative as intended better to secure "the liberties of the people . . . against the danger of standing armies in time of peace." Madison, who would later draft the Bill of Rights, supported the measure, but the convention re-jected the proposal. Mason subsequently declined to endorse the Constitution. As he explained in his frequently reprinted "Objections to This Constitution of Government," the document contained "no Declaration of Rights." Specifically, it lacked a "declaration of any kind . . . against the danger of standing armies."

Mason became an increasingly vocal opponent of ratification during the winter of 1787–1788. On the eve of Virginia's ratification convention, he joined other Antifederalists in an effort to graft the essence of the commonwealth's Article 13—along with other parts of Virginia's Bill of Rights—to the new Constitution. Declaring that the "People have a Right to keep & to bear Arms," the proposed amendment identified "a well regulated Militia [as] the proper natural and safe Defence of a free State." It also pointed to the dangers of standing armies and to the need for the "strict Subordination" of military to civil authority. A separate amendment proposed that a person "religiously scrupulous of bearing Arms" be allowed "to employ another to bear Arms in his

Stead." Neither Mason nor other members of the Antifederalist caucus gathered in Richmond criticized the Constitution's failure to guarantee individual access to weapons.

For Virginia's leading Antifederalist, the issue at hand was the militia's access to arms. "The militia may be here destroyed," Mason warned Virginia's ratification convention in a lengthy speech on June 14, 1788, "by rendering them useless, by disarming them." Great Britain had entertained a scheme some forty years before "to disarm the people . . . by totally difusing and neglecting the militia." If the new government wanted to do the same, raising a standing army in the militia's place, the states would be helpless because "congress has the exclusive right to arm them." "Why," Mason asked, "should we not provide against the danger of having our militia, our real and natural strength, destroyed?" He urged that the Constitution be amended to provide "in case the general government should neglect to arm and discipline the militia, that there should be an express declaration, that the state governments might arm and discipline them." Hence Mason backed Henry's proposal "that each State respectively shall have the Power to provide for organizing, arming and disciplining its own Militia, whensoever the Congress shall omit or neglect to provide for the Same."

The notion that the individual should be guaranteed access to weapons surfaced several times during the debate over the Constitution. The minority report of the Pennsylvania ratifying convention borrowed language from the state's own Declaration of Rights to declare the people's right "to bear arms for the defence of themselves and their own State or the United States." But it also claimed the right to bear arms "for the purpose of killing game," adding the proviso that "no law shall be passed for disarming the people or any of them." In Massachusetts, Samuel Adams argued that the Constitution be amended so to ensure that it "never [be] construed to authorize Congress to . . . prevent the people of the United States who are peaceable citizens from keeping their own arms." He later withdrew the proposal, however, probably after reflecting on the recent revolt by armed citizens in Massachusetts. Finally, New Hampshire included a proposal that "Congress shall never disarm any citizen, unless such as are or have been in actual rebellion" among a series of amendments recommended for consideration by the First Congress.

The principles evoked by those resolutions were, however, much more akin to the classical understanding of the armed citizenry than appears at first glance. Bearing arms was linked to the citizenry's collective responsibility for the republic's defense. Standard warnings about the threat of standing armies and the need to ensure the subordination of military to civil authority underscored that responsibility. Certainly neither Pennsylvania's dissenters nor New Hampshire's cautious supporters of the new constitutional arrangement had moved far, if they had moved at all, beyond the eighteenth-century notion that bearing arms meant militia service. That both states carefully qualified the individual's right to arms points to the same conclusion. New Hampshire recognized Congress's right to disarm individuals who "are or have been in actual rebellion." Pennsylvania's Antifederalists allowed the disarming of criminals. They also conceded that more inclusive measures could be enacted when society expected "real danger of public injury from individuals." Similarly, Samuel Adams's recommendation allowed for the disarming of citizens falling outside the category of "peaceable." In other words, the order and security of society took precedence over the individual's right to arms. As in more orthodox expressions of the armed citizenry's collective relationship to the political order, constitutional stability remained the preeminent consideration.

Whatever the intention of Pennsylvania and New Hampshire, no one else followed their lead while formulating either dissenting resolutions or constitutional amendments. Jefferson's recommendation that Virginia's Constitution of 1776 guarantee that no freeman be denied the use of arms "within his own lands or tenements" represents the only other hint that Americans may have viewed bearing arms as an individual right. And, of course, that language was not incorporated into the commonwealth's constitution, probably because its framers thought that the "Militia, composed of the body of the people, trained to arms," as Mason had phrased it in Article 13 of the Declaration of Rights, more accurately stated the armed citizenry's relationship to the body politic.

The amendments proposed by state ratifying conventions reflect a determination to incorporate into the new Constitution many of the principles already embodied in existing declarations of rights. New York and North Carolina, for example, urged that Congress's power to raise a peacetime army be limited by requiring "the consent of two thirds" of the House and of the Senate. Maryland even suggested that a soldier's enlistment be restricted to four years in order to prevent Congress from having access to a permanent military force. But strong state militias remained the principal means to counter the tyrannical potential of the Constitution. Seven states expressed their commitment to the citizen's right to bear arms through the agency of a well-regulated militia either through proposed amendments, general statements of principle, or in the language of dissenting resolutions. Pennsylvania's Antifederalists were the first to act; Rhode Island's tardy ratification convention was the last. The fear that the militia would be purposely neglected gave rise to proposals guaranteeing that the states could organize, arm, and discipline their citizens if Congress failed to fulfill its responsibilities. A more common fear, though, was that Congress's right to call out the militia would prove detrimental to republican liberties. New Yorkers recommended that a state's militia not be compelled to serve outside its borders longer than six weeks "without the consent of the legislature thereof." Others worried that the subjection of the militia to martial law might lead to abuses. The Maryland convention believed that "all other provisions in favor of the rights of men would be vain and nugatory, if the power of subjecting all men, able to bear arms, to martial law at any moment should remain vested in Congress." Along with North Carolina, Maryland asked Congress to amend the constitution so that the militia could be placed under martial law only "in time of war, invasion, or rebellion." Finally, several state conventions stated firmly that no person "religiously scrupulous of bearing arms" should be compelled to do military service.

Virginia's proposed amendments, which probably most directly influenced Madison's draft of the Bill of Rights, help bring into focus the concerns that ultimately produced the Second Amendment. Indeed, the changes proposed by the commonwealth's ratifying convention nicely define the issues raised during later congressional debates. Declaring that "the people have a right to keep and bear arms," Virginians asked for constitutional recognition of the principle that "a well regulated militia, composed of the body of the people trained to arms, is the proper, natural and safe defence of a free state." That proposition addressed the fear that the new government might disarm the citizenry while raising an oppressive standing army. To reinforce the point, the convention urged that the Constitution declare that standing armies "are dangerous to liberty, and therefore ought to be avoided, as far as the circumstances and protection of the community will admit." The Constitution was also found wanting for failing to pronounce the military "in all cases" subordinate to "civil power." A separate amendment urged "That any person religiously scrupulous of bearing arms ought to be exempted, upon payment of an equivalent to employ another to bear arms in his stead." At no time did anyone express concern about the right of individuals to carry weapons.

Madison had Virginia's recommendations in mind when, on June 8, 1789, he proposed to Congress that the Constitution be amended to provide that "The right of the people to keep and bear arms shall not be infringed; a well armed and well regulated militia being the best security of a free country; but no person religiously scrupulous of bearing arms shall be compelled to render military service in person." Reacting to the widely held fear that Congress's access to the militia might be misused, the Virginia representative proposed that the amendment be placed alongside the other limitations on legislative power listed in Article 1, Section 9, of the Constitution.

Six weeks later, a committee of eleven, composed of Madison and representatives from each of the other states that had ratified the Constitution, began preparing a formal slate of amendments, using as a guide both Madison's recommendations and those proposed by the states. The committee revised Madison's original recommendation, stating more explicitly the armed citizenry's importance to the constitutional order. "A well regulated militia, composed of the body of the people," the new language read, "being the best security of a free state, the right of the people to keep and bear arms shall not be infringed." The use of the term *people* in the collective sense is unmistakable here. Madison's proposal to guarantee for individuals the free exercise of conscience in military matters was rewritten as well. The committee recommended that "no person religiously scrupulous shall be compelled to bear arms," removing even the obligation to pay an "equivalent" in lieu of military service.

Most members of Congress found the committee's recommendation acceptable. The doubts that were raised underscore the aim of the Second Amendment to guarantee the militia's place under the new constitutional order. Elbridge Gerry commented that only the feared "mal-administration of the Government" made such an amendment necessary. He suggested that rephrasing the proposal to read "a well regulated militia, trained to arms" might better accomplish the desired end, making it "the duty of the Government to provide this security." "Whenever Governments mean to invade the rights and liberties of the people," he reminded the House, "they always attempt to destroy the militia, in order to raise an army upon their ruins."

Gerry's proposal failed to receive a second and died on the House floor, but his related concern that the exemption for conscientious objectors might seriously undermine the viability of the militia received a far more sympathetic hearing. The government might declare every citizen "religiously scrupulous, and prevent them from bearing arms," leaving the citizenry defenseless against a standing army, Gerry warned. His fear no doubt struck most in the hall as a bit farfetched. Still, the amendment's failure to link freedom of conscience to the obligation to find a substitute or to pay an "equivalent" troubled many members of the House. Requiring one part of the population to provide for the defense of the other was simply "unjust," argued Georgia's James Jackson. Others believed that matters of "religious persuasion" had no place in an amendment designed to guarantee a fundamental principle of republican government. "It is extremely injudicious," warned one congressman, "to intermix matters of doubt with fundamentals." Together those concerns caused the House to come within two votes of striking the conscientious objection clause from the proposed amendment.

Yet another concern arose on the House floor before the amendment was passed on to the Senate. It spoke to a feeling, frequently expressed in state declarations of rights, that guaranteeing a place for the militia in the constitutional order would not alone prevent abuse of Congress's prerogative to raise standing armies. South Carolina's Aedanus Burke asked for a clause declaring that a "standing army . . . in time of peace is dangerous to public liberty, and such shall not be raised . . . without the consent of two-thirds of the members present of both Houses." He also asked for an explicit statement of the subordination of military to civil authority. The amendment received a second but was defeated after objections were raised to requiring more than a majority vote and amid complaints that debate had already been closed. Nevertheless, Burke's amendment underscores the context in which Congress debated the Second Amendment. The aim was to lay down a fundamental principle of republican government: that a well-regulated militia was the "best security of a free state."

Little is known about the Senate's debate of the Second Amendment, though it seems to have followed a pattern similar to that in the House. The controversial conscientious objection clause failed to get Senate approval. The body, however, joined the House in rejecting a proposal to restrict Congress's power to raise armies during peacetime. Finally, the Senate rejected an amendment to insert "for the common defence"—apparently after "to bear arms"—while it agreed to rephrase the nature of the militia's relationship to the Republic's security, calling it "necessary to," rather than the "best" form of, national defense. The first change no doubt reflected efforts to ensure that it was the militia that was to bear arms; its rejection reflected not the undesirability of that end but, rather, the feeling that the proposal was redundant. The decision to describe the militia as necessary to the national defense more accurately expressed the growing sentiment in America that in wartime regular soldiers also had an important role to play, even in the defense of a republic.

The Senate's changes were accepted by a joint conference committee of both houses, and on September 24 and September 25, 1789, the House and Senate respectively voted their approval. Unfortunately, we know little about the Second Amendment's reception in the states. No state rejected the amendment. As a statement of republican principle already commonplace in many state declarations of rights, it probably evoked little discussion. If doubts were raised, and there is no evidence that they were, they probably centered on the amendment's failure to link the militia explicitly to the dangers represented by a standing army.

Whatever the issues, when Virginia ratified the Second Amendment on December 15, 1791, "A well regulated Militia, being necessary to the security of a free State, the right of the people to keep and bear Arms, shall not be infringed" became part of the Constitution. The notion that republicanism depended on a vital militia had become part of the nation's higher law. Henceforth, Congress was prohibited from taking any action that might disarm or otherwise render the militia less effective. The Second Amendment, then, stated a basic principle of American republicanism: The body politic's ability to defend the liberties of the people and the constitutional foundation of the state against an ambitious tyrant's standing army or a manipulative demagogue's armed mob could not be infringed upon.

Through the early national period, the trained militiaman remained linked to constitutional stability and to the liberty that that ensured. "A people [can] defend their territory, or resist an assuming government," reminded Thomas Barnard in a 1789 sermon addressing the importance of a well-disciplined militia, "but by arms." The members of the Ancient and Honorable Artillery Company in attendance could not have found his counsel surprising. Though frustrated by the performance of militia soldiers during the war years, few Americans—including the Continental Army's principal training officer, Friedrich von Steuben—questioned the desirability of having "a perfect knowledge of the duties of a soldier engraved on the mind of every citizen." And most would have agreed that only a well-organized militia could accomplish that end. Henry Knox, also formerly among George Washington's chief advisers, believed that the "future glory and power of the United States" depended on the establishment of a militia structure that not only trained citizens to arms but also instilled a commitment to the public good. As the last secretary at war to serve under the Articles of Confederation, he proposed such a plan—a plan he thought capable "of forming the manners of the rising generation on principles of republican virtue; of infusing into their minds, that the love of their country, and the knowledge of defending it, are political duties of the most indispensible nature."

At Washington's request, Knox in early 1790 submitted to Congress a revised version of his plan for militia reform, prefaced by remarks that reveal much about the assumptions behind the ratification of the Second Amendment. The United States, Knox wrote, had an "invaluable opportunity" to establish "such institutions as shall invigorate, exalt, and perpetuate, the great principles of freedom." The militia was one such institution: "an efficient military branch of Government can[not] be invented, with safety to the great principles of liberty, unless the same shall be formed of the people themselves, and supported by their habits and manners." Simply put, "an energetic national militia is to be regarded as the capital security of a free Republic; and not a standing army." In the first place, "every man . . . is firmly bound by the social compact to perform, personally, his proportion of military duty for the defence of the State." On a more practical level, however, the security of a free society depended on the people's possessing "a competent knowledge of the military art"—a knowledge that could be "attained in the present state of society" only by establishing adequate institutions for military education.

Basing the "responsib[ility] for different degrees of military service" on age and physical ability, Knox proposed a classed militia intended to prepare citizens to meet both their military and their civil responsibilities. The external and internal security of the nation would be ensured by the arms of "the well-informed members of the community, actuated by the highest motives." Indeed, the citizen-soldier and the body politic would be indistinguishable under Knox's scheme. Certification of militia service would be "required as an indispensable qualification for exercising any of the rights of a free citizen." His militia plan, Knox believed, would have far-reaching consequences for America: "an energetic republican militia [would] be durably established, the invaluable principles of liberty secured and perpetuated, and a dignified national fabric erected on the solid foundation of public virtue."

Knox's attempt to institutionalize, through the militia, classical perceptions of the corporate character of society as well as the importance of public virtue proved too ambitious. Many congressmen, fearing the consequences of granting the national government extensive control over local militia units, preferred instead to establish a decentralized militia system that reflected long-standing American concerns about centralized military authority. Few legislators, though, questioned the values Knox's militia plan was intended to instill. "The security of a free State," to use the language of the Second Amendment, depended on an armed citizenry formed into "a well regulated Militia." Indeed, when Americans spoke of the armed citizenry's role in the preservation of liberty, they assumed a vital militia founded on classical notions of citizenship.

The debate over militia reform that followed on the heels of the Whisky Rebellion is a case in point. The militia had proved less than energetic in the face of western Pennsylvania's insurgency. More troubling was that the men who came out were not, as Jeremiah Wadsworth put it, "the militia of the law." They were but volunteers "influenced by their feelings, or by private bounties." That the insurrection had been put down missed the point. A republic must depend on its citizenry to recognize and to respond to assaults on its security. "For any Government to rely on private, individual influence, to protect it against its enemies, whether foreign or domestic," was dangerous. "The same influence," advised Wadsworth, "may be turned against the Government." William Findley, a leading Republican from Pennsylvania, also found disconcerting the militia's reputation "as an undisciplined band of substitutes, induced to undertake the service by the receipt of bounty and the expectation of plunder." The mobilized militia should reflect the body politic, each citizen "discharging [his] duty in obedience to the laws, on the same principles with a court, jury or sheriff." After all, the militia "are as much the representatives of the citizens, when they are called to support the laws of their country, as the members of Congress are their Representatives to make those laws."

Similar concerns surfaced with the addition of the volunteer corps to the American military establishment during the quasi war with France. In Congress, Republicans charged that drawing on "men of a particular cast"—those able to arm, to clothe, and to equip themselves—to serve at the president's behest would undermine the constitutional balance guaranteed by the citizen militia. Specifically, the volunteer corps reduced military service to an expression of partisan sentiment, setting the armed force of government apart from the body politic. The militiaman, "regulated by law," defended liberty; but individuals united under arms by the passions of the moment threatened the constitutional order and the freedom it preserved. As the citizens of Louisa County, Virginia, stated the issue—using language repeated again and again by those who feared for the constitutional stability of the Republic—"a well regulated and well organized militia, as immediately connecting the duties of citizens and soldiers, are the surest safeguard to the rights and liberties of the people." If the Federalists had their way, warned one "Humanus," the consequences would be "a well armed party-corps . . . on the one hand; and a neglected, difused, and un-armed militia, on the other."

The discussion evoked by John Randolph's recommendation in 1807 that Congress provide "by law, for arming and equipping the whole body of the militia of the United States" also sheds light on what contemporaries meant by "the right of the people to keep and bear Arms." "An armed people must necessarily be a free people," argued Randolph while calling for the systematic arming of all militiamen. Few in Congress disagreed. Indeed, most probably concurred with Pennsylvania's John Smilie when he observed that "it was undoubtedly a melancholy consideration, that a people enjoying the first privileges of freemen, had not yet availed themselves of one of their most important rights, that of arming themselves." Opposition that did arise centered on the practical question of cost and on the ideologically inspired fear that a militia armed by the federal government might be disarmed by the same authority. James Fisk predicted that "in the same proportion as the General Government furnished arms to the people, in the same proportion would their patriotic zeal to furnish themselves with arms be lessened." Nevertheless, his fear that Randolph's plan would jeopardize "the liberties of the people" emphasizes that for Americans the armed citizenry, "the people," were synonymous with "a well regulated Militia." "It [is] a correct principle," announced John Rhea of Tennessee, "that all the militia should be armed under a Republican Government. One of the objects of such a Government was, that the people should have arms in their hands." Roger Nelson of Maryland supported the plan to arm the militia because "he wished the people . . . to be prepared at all times to repel encroachments on their rights and liberties, whether internal or external."

When discussions during the early national period turned to the preservation of liberty, then, classical assumptions about the citizen's responsibility to bear arms in the interest of the common good quickly came to the fore. "For a people who are free, and who mean to remain so," Jefferson reminded Congress in 1808 in language that summarized the republican principles embodied in the Second Amendment, "a well organized and armed militia is their best security." No one argued that the individual had a right to bear arms outside the ranks of the militia. To the contrary, bearing arms outside the framework of the established militia structure immediately provoked fears for the constitutional stability of the Republic.

Certainly there was no doubt in the mind of Justice Joseph Story, the great constitutional commentator of the period, that the Second Amendment was intended to guarantee "a well regulated militia." "The importance of this article will scarcely be doubted by any persons who have duly reflected upon the subject." Why? Because "the militia is the natural defence of a free country against sudden foreign invasions, domestic insurrections, and domestic usurpations of power by rulers." Citing Sir William Blackstone's *Commentaries of the Laws of England*, Story noted that "the right of the citizens to keep and bear arms has justly been considered, as the palladium of the liberties of a republic; since it offers a strong moral check against the usurpation and arbitrary power of rulers." Story's only concern was that Americans had developed an indifference to the militia that he feared would lead to contempt. If that happened, "all the protection intended by this clause of our national bill of rights" would be undermined. "The importance of a well regulated militia would seem so undeniable," argued the Supreme Court justice, that "how it is practicable to keep the people duly armed without some organization, it is difficult to see."

The state and federal courts have seldom wavered from Story's interpretation of the Second Amendment. Thomas M. Cooley's 1884 edition of Blackstone's *Commentaries on the Laws of England* includes an annotation to the English jurist's comments on the right to bear arms, the annotation stating that "in the United States this right is preserved by express constitutional provisions. But it extends no further than to keep and bear those arms which are suited and proper for the general defense of the community against invasion and oppression." The decision handed down by the New Jersey Supreme Court a century later is typical of what is by now nearly two centuries of constitutional opinion solidly based in the intellectual climate of the eighteenth century: "The Second Amendment, concerning the right of the people to keep and bear arms, was framed in contemplation not of individual rights but of the maintenance of the states' active, organized militias."

THE SECOND AMENDMENT
AND THE RIGHT TO BEAR ARMS: AN EXCHANGE[3]

To the Editor of the *Journal of American History:*

Prompted by the current debate over gun control, a number of scholars have explored the origins of the Second Amendment to the Constitution. Depending on their view of the contemporary controversy over gun legislation, some see the true meaning of the amendment in its right to bear arms phrase, while others insist that the communal prerogatives implied in its well-regulated militia clause reveal the Founders' actual intent. Lawrence Delbert Cress joins the fray on the side of those committed to community prerogatives (*Journal of American History*, Vol. 71, June 1984). In the process, he has questioned my interpretation (*Journal of American History*, Vol. 69, December 1982) of the issues involved. I believe the main differences between us stem from Cress's contention that the Founding Fathers would never have argued "that the individual had a right to bear arms outside the ranks of the militia." Leaving aside the fact that Cress does not adequately explain how the Founding Fathers could possibly have advocated an armed militia without also providing for an armed citizenry from which the militia would be drawn, I disagree with him at two points: (1) It seems to me that his understanding of the political culture of eighteenth-century America is naive; and (2) it seems to me that while the Founders *did*, in fact, put great stress on the existence of a militia (although not for precisely the reasons that Cress argues), they also made a place in their thinking for the right of individual republican citizens to keep and to bear arms apart from service in the militia.

Cress grounds his argument on the Founding Fathers' belief in republicanism, suggesting "that seventeenth- and eighteenth-century republican theorists understood access to arms to be a communal, rather than an individual, right." Cress takes quite se-

[3]Reprint of an article by Robert E. Shalhope, professor of history at the University of Oklahoma, and Lawrence Delbert Cress, associate professor of history at Texas A & M University. Reprinted by permission from *The Journal of American History*, Vol. 71 (D. '84), pp. 587–93. Copyright © 1984 by *The Journal of American History*.

riously—and quite literally—the republican language of the day, and he treats republican rhetoric as an entirely accurate reflection of the reality of the period. For him, "citizenship . . . connoted civic virtue, a commitment to the greater public good, not an insistence on individual prerogative." Then: "As had Machiavelli, Harrington, and the radical Whigs, Americans saw the militia as an expression of the corporate unity of society. Men of rank and substance commanded the 'well regulated' militia; men of lesser means filled its rank and file. In short, the parade field reinforced the deferential social and political relationships that ensured order and a respect for authority throughout society." In Cress's opinion, republican language and literature reveal an organic world typified by a deferential citizen who willingly subordinated individual interests to the common good. Thus, the Second Amendment represented "the classical republican notion" that arms bearing was solely a corporate function.

An increasing body of literature dealing with eighteenth-century America raises serious questions about such an interpretation. Kenneth A. Lockridge, Edmund S. Morgan, Gary B. Nash, Gordon S. Wood, Philip J. Greven, Jr., Joyce Appleby, and good many other portray an increasingly complex society undergoing important transformations, a society filled with tension and anxieties. In light of this research, Cress's interpretation of the militia as "an expression of the corporate unity of society" as well as his treatment of republican citizenship as connoting "civic virtue, a commitment to the greater public good"—the very foundation of his interpretation of the origins of the Second Amendment—appears naive and simplistic. Observations by Appleby and Wood exemplify the thrust of this recent research. For her part, Appleby maintains that "a social order of due subordination incumbent in varying degrees upon all members of the community gave way in the decades after 1730 to an atomized society." She shows that colonial America underwent a modernizing process that gave rise to "the aggressive individualism, the optimistic materialism, and the pragmatic interest-group politics that became so salient so early in the life of the new nation." Wood, too, sees the destruction of the corporate society idealized by classical republican literature. He notes that at the time of the Revolution, "the people were not an order organically tied together by their unity of interest but rather an agglomeration of hostile individuals coming together for their mutual benefit to

construct a society." Thus, "instead of inculcating a new respect
for order, simplicity, and selflessness, republicanism was breed-
ing disorder, extravagance, and individualism." Observing that
the idea of the organic community had become a cliché during
the eighteenth century, Wood points out that "the very fact that
the social basis for such a corporate ideal had long been disinte-
grating, if it ever existed, only accentuated its desirability in
American eyes." Caught up in a society of rampant materialism
and strident individualism, many Americans idealized the corporate society in their speech and writing, but such rhetoric belied
American experience.

The insights of Wood and others escape Cress. Instead, his
portrayal of republican citizenship and the militia confuses the
ideal for which so many Americans spoke with the reality of their
actual existence. Fortunately, not every scholar who has dealt
with the militia has fallen into this error. Charles Royster, in his
A Revolutionary People at War, offers a much more sophisticated
understanding of the militia in revolutionary America. He contends that while many Americans entered the Revolution filled
with the millennial expectation of creating a virtuous republican
society during the course of the war, American behavior mani-
fested disturbing and disappointing signs of European vices. Most
important, the militia—the backbone of an idealized republican
society—proved ineffective; only the presence of a professional
army saved the cause. And yet, following Yorktown, Americans
chose to believe that their victory was confirmation of their moral
strengths. To hold on to their millennial vision of the future, the
revolutionary generation redefined its experiences and made
them as virtuous and as heroic as they ought to have been. Americans offered the noble standard of 1775 and the image of a uni-
fied, virtuous republican citizenry to future generations. This
impulse helps to explain the exaggerated significance accorded
the militia by Americans in the 1780s. Thus, when the Founders
drafted the Bill of Rights, they responded to an environment
filled with hyperbolic praise of the militia. Historians should not,
however, confuse rhetoric with reality. A great many Americans
may well have desired their militia to reinforce "the deferential
social and political relationships that ensured order and a respect
for authority throughout society," but they knew better.

The work of Royster, Wood, and others indicates that the
Second Amendment emerged within a culture characterized by

individualistic strivings and aggressive materialism, deeply concerned with individual rights as well as with communal responsibilities. James Madison, for example, having buttressed the corporate nature of society with the Constitution, set out to protect the individual from the potentially overweening power of the community. He worried lest it "be thought all paper barriers against the power of the community, are too weak to be worthy of attention" but, nonetheless, forged ahead. When he offered the amendments comprising the Bill of Rights, Madison suggested that they be inserted directly into the body of the Constitution in Article 1, Section 9, between clauses three and four. He did not separate the right to bear arms from the other rights designed to protect the individual; he did not suggest placing it in Section 8, clauses fifteen and sixteen, which dealt specifically with arming and organizing the militia. When he prepared notes for an address supporting the amendments, Madison reminded himself: "They relate 1st to private rights." And when he consulted with Edmund Pendleton, he emphasized that "amendments may be employed to quiet the fears of many by supplying those further guards for private rights." Madison's confidant, Joseph Jones, believed the proposed articles "are calculated to secure the personal rights of the people so far as declarations on paper can effect the purpose." Tench Coxe, writing as "Pennsylvanian," discussed individual guarantees and then, in reference to the Second Amendment, maintained that "the people are confirmed by the next article in their right to keep and bear their private arms." "Philodemos" exclaimed: "Every freeman has a right to the use of the press, so he has to *the use of his arms.*"

Interpreting the origins of the Second Amendment is a difficult task, because it forces scholars to evaluate the political culture of late-eighteenth-century America. To understand fully the political culture of any society, however, is not easy, because, as Louis Wirth so cogently observed, "the most elemental and important facts about a society are those that are seldom debated and generally regarded as settled." John Stuart Mill also understood that "the obvious and universal facts, which every one sees and no one is astonished at, it seldom occurs to any one to place upon record; and posterity, if it learn the rule, learns it, generally, from the notice bestowed by contemporaries on some accidental exception." Thus, historians must not be too quick to repeat the most widely broadcast statements of a time and to conclude that those tell us all we need to know. Royster makes it very clear why Americans were constantly lauding their militias, and, at the same time, his work reveals that to take such statements at face value, particularly as the motivating force behind the Second Amendment, obscures more than it clarifies. Subtler statements afford access to those beliefs that Americans quietly considered "settled" and beyond the necessity of debate.

In their attempt to contrast the strengths of America with the decadence of Europe, Americans ofttimes revealed their assumptions about the place of arms in their society. Madison, in the *Federalist* No. 46, noted "the advantages of being armed, which the Americans possess over the people of almost every other nation." Then he observed that in Europe "the governements are afraid to trust the people with arms." Years later Timothy Dwight testified to the strength and durability of this belief when he boasted that "to trust arms in the hands of the people at large has, in Europe, been believed . . . to be an experiment fraught only with danger." By contrast, in America "few men will be disposed to use arms, unless for their amusement, and for the defence of themselves and their country." Joel Barlow, however, most eloquently articulated the vital role of arms in American republican thought. He insisted that any government that disarmed its people "palsies the hand and brutalizes the mind: an habitual disuse of physical forces totally destroys the moral; and men lose at once the power of protecting themselves, and of discerning the cause of their oppression." To republicans, a dynamic relationship existed between the possession of arms and the virile, independent citizen considered the basis of America's superiority over Europe.

The statements of Barlow and others indicate that Americans considered the armed citizen central to the character of their society. But what, exactly, was the nature of the relationship between arms and the character of the American citizen? Here Thomas Jefferson provides important insight. In an initial draft of a proposed constitution for the state of Virginia, Jefferson did not mention a militia at all. Nevertheless, he did insist that "no freeman shall ever be debarred the use of arms." He amended this statement in his next two drafts to read: "No freeman shall be debarred the use of arms within his own lands or tenements." Clearly, Jefferson considered the possession of arms entirely unrelated to service in the militia. But, then, what link existed between such possession and the republican character? In a letter to his nephew, Peter Carr, Jefferson offered a bit of advice regarding exercise. It is one of Mill's little "accidental exceptions" that help to illuminate the political culture of an age. Jefferson advised Carr that a few hours each day should be set aside for physical exertion. "As to the species of exercise, I advise the gun. While this gives a moderate exercise to the body, it gives boldness, enterprize, and independance to the mind." Further, he claimed: "Games played with the ball and others of that nature, are too violent for the body and stamp no character on the mind. Let your gun therefore be the constant companion of your walks."

It is clear that Americans living in the late eighteenth century took for granted the individual's right to possess arms. It is equally clear that, for a variety of reasons, they also insisted on the right to maintain local militias. More often than not they considered these rights inseparable. This raises the question of why these two things were so often intertwined as to make it seem natural to combine them in the Second Amendment. Here comments by Madison, Dwight, and Joseph Story are particularly illuminating.

Madison observed, of the oppressed Europeans, that "it is not certain that with this aid alone [possession of arms], they would not be able to shake off their yokes." Something beyond individual possession of weapons was necessary: "But were the people to possess the additional advantages of local governements chosen by themselves, who could collect the national will, and direct the national force; and of officers appointed out of the militia, by these governments and attached both to them and to the militia, it may be affirmed with the greatest assurance, that the throne of every tyranny in Europe would be speedily overturned, in spite of the legions which surround it." Writing early in the nineteenth century, Dwight celebrated the right of individuals to possess arms as the hallmark of a democratic society. Then, he concluded: "The difficulty here has been to persuade the citizens to keep arms, not to prevent them from being employed for violent purposes." This same lament coursed through the observation of Story, whose *Commentaries on the Constitution of the United States* summed up the relationship between armed citizens and the militia as clearly as it was ever stated. In his discussion of the Second Amendment, Story claimed that the "right of the citizens to keep and bear arms has justly been considered, as the palladium of the liberties of a republic." And yet, even "though this truth would seem so clear, and the importance of a well regulated militia would seem so undeniable, it cannot be disguised, that among the American people there is a growing indifference to any system of militia discipline, and a strong disposition, from a sense of its bur- thens, to be rid of all regulations." Then Story expressed his cen- tral concern: "How it is practicable to keep the people duly armed without some organization, it is difficult to see."

Madison, Dwight, and Story firmly believed that the charac- ter and spirit of the Republic rested on the individual freeman's possession of arms as well as on his ability and willingness to defend himself and his society. This was the bedrock, the "palladium," of republican liberty. The militia was equally impor- tant in their minds. Militia laws insured that freemen would re- main armed, and thus vigorous republican citizens. In addition, the militia served as the means whereby the collective force of in- dividually armed citizens might become effective. It was this that would cause those in power to respect the liberties of the people. This belief lay behind Jefferson's oft-quoted words: "What coun- try can preserve it's liberties if their rulers are not warned from time to time that their people preserve the spirit of resistance? Let them take arms." Thus, the armed citizen and the militia ex- isted as distinct, yet dynamically interrelated, elements within American thought, and it was perfectly reasonable to provide for both within the same amendment to the Constitution.

It may very well be true that *neither* the militia nor the armed citizen is appropriate for modern society. This is a matter to be decided by our courts and our legislatures. In any event, we must not allow today's needs, however urgently they are felt, to ob- scure our understanding of the Second Amendment and, in the process, our understanding of revolutionary America. The Sec- ond Amendment included *both* of its provisions because the Founders intended that both of them be taken seriously. They meant to balance as best they could individual rights with commu- nal responsibilities.

ROBERT E. SHALHOPE
UNIVERSITY OF OKLAHOMA

To the Editor of the *Journal of American History:*

I am pleased to see the interest that my article has generated. My differences with Robert E. Shalhope's view of the origins and significance of the Second Amendment have already been made clear *(Journal of American History,* Vol. 71, June 1984). Readers will have to judge for themselves which interpretation is more faithful to the documents.

Let me say here only that Shalhope's charcterization of the late eighteenth century as a period of increasing individualism in no way contradicts my interpretation of the origins and meaning of the Second Amendment. The works of Gordon S. Wood, Joyce Appleby, and others offer insights into the dynamic character of revolutionary society with which I have no disagreement. Neither would I disagree with Charles Royster's interpretation of the militia in revolutionary America. In fact, as Royster quite clearly shows, Americans clung desperately to the ideals of the militia even in the face of its failure. "The preeminent popular message of 1783 was the triumph of public virtue, not its failure," Royster writes. Public virtue may have been passé, as Shalhope claims, but that troubled Americans. The Second Amendment was an attempt to provide an institutional framework capable of ensuring a virtuous citizenry.

Shalhope believes a tumultuous and increasingly individualistic society to be incapable of espousing constitutional principles founded in communitarian values. I disagree. The Second Amendment was founded in classical republican notions of the obligations inherent in citizenship. Those ideas may have been anachronistic in 1789, but they are a clear reflection of the lingering influence of what J. G. A. Pocock has called the "Machiavellian Moment."

None of this is to deny that the constitutional right of individuals to own guns did not surface in the late eighteenth century. I have cited several examples myself. But these were minority views clearly out of touch with prevailing constitutional theory. Common sense alone would suggest that a society that was unwilling to allow all adult males to vote would not embrace a constitutional principle ensuring their right to own firearms.

Finally, I share completely Shalhope's sentiment that "we must not allow today's needs, however urgently they are felt, to obscure our understanding of the origins of the Second Amendment."

LAWRENCE DELBERT CRESS
TEXAS A&M UNIVERSITY

SHOOTING DOWN GUN MYTHS[4]

The media event that began on Dec. 22, 1984, when subway rider Bernhard Hugo Goetz responded to a demand for $5 from four youths with bullets from a .38-caliber revolver serves as a recent reminder that what historian Richard Hofstadter once labeled the "gun culture" is still tightly woven into the fabric of the American psyche. Much has been written about the political and criminological consequences of gun control, including the proliferation of weapons (especially cheap handguns), the effectiveness or ineffectiveness of various gun control measures and the almost staggering influence of the National Rifle Association in preventing stricter gun laws.

Yet there has been surprisingly little public examination of the central constitutional question pertaining to guns—namely, the meaning of the Second Amendment: "A well regulated militia being necessary to the security of a free state, the right of the people to keep and bear arms shall not be infringed." The oft-repeated cry of gun control opponents extolling the so-called individual "right to keep and bear arms" has been accepted by most of the public (a 1978 survey reported that 88 percent of Americans believe they have an individual right to bear arms) in large part because it has often and stridently been repeated. A simple examination of how the courts have interpreted the Second Amendment shows, however, that those who think the Constitution gives them a right to tote a gun have not got a leg to stand on.

The Second Amendment admittedly has not received as much of the Supreme Court's attention over the years as have other Bill of Rights issues, like free speech, free press and the right to counsel. But four cases provide the basis for understanding the Supreme Court's thinking on the matter over the last century.

[4]Reprint of an article by Robert Spitzer, chairman of the political science department at the State University of New York at Cortland. Reprinted by permission from *America*, Je. 8, '85, pp. 468-69. Copyright © 1985 by *America*.

The first Supreme Court ruling on the Second Amendment occurred in a case called U.S. v. Cruikshank (1876). Speaking for the Court, Chief Justice Morrison R. Waite said the right "of bearing arms for a lawful purpose is not a right granted by the Constitution, nor is it in any manner dependent upon that instrument for its existence." The Cruikshank case established two principles: First, the Second Amendment does not afford an individual right to bear arms (as distinct from an individual's participation in a collective body or militia); second, the Second Amendment is not legally "incorporated"—that is, does not apply to the states through the due process and equal protection clauses of the 14th Amendment. The concept of "incorporation" is highly important in understanding the scope of the Second Amendment and the Bill of Rights as a whole. The process of incorporation has been the means by which the courts have extended constitutional protections to individuals in non-Federal cases. In 1876, none of the Bill of Rights had been incorporated; today, however, most of the constitutional protections we take for granted, like protection from unreasonable searches and seizures and the rights of free assembly and free exercise of religion, protect us because the Supreme Court "incorporated" them. The Court has never, however, "incorporated" the Second Amendment.

The second important court case was Presser v. Illinois (1886). In that case, the Court reaffirmed Cruikshank, and stated that the Second Amendment does not apply to the states (is not "incorporated") and affirmed that though the states have the right to form militias, they are also free to regulate the circumstances under which citizens bear arms, within the parameters of state constitutions.

In an 1894 case, Miller v. Texas, the Supreme Court upheld the right of states to regulate arms and said again that the Second Amendment did not apply to the states. The fourth and most important case came in 1939. U.S. v. Miller involved a challenge to Federal gun regulations stemming from the National Firearms Act of 1934. Speaking for a unanimous Court, Justice James C. McReynolds affirmed the right of the Federal Government to regulate firearms (in particular, transport and possession) and stated unambiguously that citizens possess a constitutional right to bear arms only in connection with service in a militia. Justice Miller also cited the Cruikshank and Presser cases as precedent, affirming the principles articulated in those cases.

The continued pertinence of the Miller case is indicated by two other recent Supreme Court cases. In a 1972 case, Adams v. Williams, Justices William O. Douglas and Thurgood Marshall issued a joint dissent in which they cited Miller and affirmed their view that the state could regulate firearms as it saw fit. The case itself, however, did not deal with the Second Amendment. In 1980, Justice Harry A. Blackmun commented in a footnote to his majority opinion (Lewis v. U.S.) that the Miller case represented the Court's thinking on gun control.

One final case warrants mention, though it was not reviewed by the Supreme Court. On June 8, 1981, the village of Morton Grove, Ill., enacted an ordinance that banned the possession of handguns, except for police, prison officials, the military, collectors and others needing guns for their work. Residents who owned guns could keep and use them in licensed gun clubs, however. The ordinance was challenged by the National Rifle Association and their sympathizers. Both Federal District Court and the Federal Court of Appeals rejected the arguments of the ordinance opponents. Both Federal courts said that the Second Amendment did not apply to the states, that there was no individual right to bear arms, that the Morton Grove ordinance was a reasonable exercise of authority and that the right to bear arms applies only to the maintenance of a well regulated militia (as was said in Miller).

The case of Quilici v. Village of Morton Grove was appealed to the Supreme Court, but it declined to hear the case, leaving the lower Federal court ruling as the operative interpretation.

This recitation of cases demonstrates the Court's long recognition of the right of the Government to regulate the ownership and use of firearms as it sees fit. The fact that sweeping national regulations have not been enacted is not due to a lack of constitutional authority, but rather to the political clout of gun control opponents and a gun "mythology" perpetuated in large part by gun enthusiasts.

Even if we examine the intentions of the founding fathers, it is clear that their considerations in authorizing the Second Amendment lay with national defense. The citizen militia was considered the military force least threatening to democratic values and institutions. They feared the baneful consequences of a regular standing army, as European and earlier American history were replete with examples of tyrannies extended by such armies. Despite these fears, the founding fathers were also well aware of the military limitations of an army composed of part-time soldiers, and provision was made in the Constitution (Article I, Section 8) for both a militia and a standing army. The role of the citizen militia was formally supplanted in 1916 by the National Defense Act, which recognized the National Guard as the militia. And, of course, early fears of a standing army that would overthrow American democratic institutions never materialized.

Thus, the Second Amendment protects a "right to keep and bear arms" only for service in a "well regulated militia" that has not been called up since the beginning of the 19th century. As Bill of Rights scholar Irving Brant observed, the Second Amendment "comes to life chiefly on the parade floats of rifle associations and in the propaganda of mail-order houses selling pistols to teen-age gangsters."

Many have applauded the actions of Bernhard Goetz as legitimate self-defense, or as justifiable vigilantism. But even if we accept the propriety of his actions, how do we disentangle his "right" to carry and use a gun from the less ambiguous case of James Alan Kearbey, a 14-year-old junior high school student who, on Jan. 21, entered his Goddard, Kan., school with an M-1 rifle and a .357 magnum pistol (popularized in Clint Eastwood's film "Dirty Harry"). Kearbey shot and killed the school principal and wounded three others. Goddard English teacher Darlene Criss ironically described the town as "the safest place in America."

The Goetz case and the Kearbey case both argue for Government to exercise its right to regulate the possession and use of firearms. But as the merits of gun control are debated, it is time that we once and for all excised erroneous references to an individual, constitutionally based "right" to bear arms.

II. DEBATE AND LEGISLATION

EDITOR'S INTRODUCTION

The second section of this volume concerns the debate between pro- and anti-gun lobbies and legislation adopted by Congress in the 1980s. The first selection, by Jervis Anderson, is an excerpt from an article in *The New Yorker*, subsequently incorporated into his book *Guns in American Life* (1984), that reviews federal gun laws from the 1930s onward, and the principal gun lobbies in the U. S. The effect of the Gun Control Act in the 1960s, as Anderson notes, was to galvanize the National Rifle Association, until then a recreational association of sportsmen and hunters, into a strong pro-gun lobby whose effect on subsequent legislation—at federal, state, and local levels—has been profound. The various gun lobbies, both for and against restrictions on guns, are also described by Anderson. In four following articles, the gun lobbies speak for themselves. Two pamphlets each by Handgun Control, Inc. and the National Rifle Association set forth the nature of their organizations and their opposing attitudes toward the gun control issue.

In a following article, an editorial from *The New Republic* comments on President Reagan's address to the NRA convention and his endorsement of the organization's views. It is followed by a partial transcript, from the *Congressional Digest*, of the debate in Congress over the McClure-Volkmer Bill, relaxing restrictions on the sale and ownership of handguns. Those speaking in support of the bill include Robert Dole, James McClure, and Orrin Hatch, while those in opposition include Edward Kennedy, Charles Mathias, and Christopher Dodd.

The record of the debate is followed by two articles, an editorial from the *New Republic* and an article by William R. Doerner from *Time*, that explain the outcome of the issue—the voting down of Senator Kennedy's proposed amendment to ease regulations on hunting and sporting rifles while retaining them for handguns, and the adoption of the McClure-Volkmer Bill in its substantially undiluted form.

are often based on New York State's Sullivan Law, which is one of the oldest and strictest handgun statutes in the country, and which has been a popular target for those who argue that gun laws don't work. But that argument overlooks the fact that most illegal handguns in New York are purchased in states where there are looser gun laws, or from residents of such states who bring handguns into New York and sell them here.) The President might not have read the F.B.I.'s "Crime in the United States" for 1981, which discloses the following: "When the number of murder victims was related to the regional populations, the most populous Southern States averaged 13 murders per 100,000 people. . . . The Western States [had] a murder rate of 10 per 100,000. . . . The Northeastern States experienced a . . . murder rate [of] 8 per 100,000 population. The North Central States had a rate of 7 victims per 100,000 inhabitants." One point the F.B.I. report failed to make, since crime statistics are its main interest, is that the Northeastern states, with one of the lower murder rates per capita, also have some of the tougher gun laws in the country. Nor can it be concluded, from what the 1981 CBS documentary revealed about teen-age gun violence in Los Angeles, that the tough prison sentences enacted during Reagan's tenure as governor of California are having the deterrent effect they were intended to have.

Since the early seventies, when it became clear that dealers were circumventing the Gun Control Act of 1968, a number of bills have been introduced in Congress to close the loopholes and stiffen the act. Almost all have died or been snarled in committee. Pro-gun legislators not only helped to stymie those bills but also introduced some of their own. At the moment, there are two major gun proposals, one from each camp. One of them, whose co-authors are Senator Edward Kennedy and Representive Peter Rodino, proposes a ban on the domestic manufacture of cheap handguns and on the importation of parts that are used to assemble Saturday-night specials. The other, whose co-authors are Senator James McClure and Representative Harold Volkmer, and which is known as the Firearms Owners Protection Act, seeks, in effect, to pull whatever teeth are left in the Gun Control Act of 1968. Even in the House, which has been controlled by the Democrats, there is little enthusiasm for Kennedy-Rodino, whereas McClure-Volkmer has been co-sponsored by a majority in the Republican-controlled Senate, and President Reagan has promised to sign it if it comes to his desk. As a 1982 Senate document, "Federal Regulation of Firearms," states, "Thus, on the subject of violent crime, there remains a clear division in Congress between advocates of an interdiction solution—a policy that seeks to lessen the likelihood and danger of crime by curbing access to the more lethal weapons—and those who believe the problem is one of establishing a more effective system of criminal justice. The former see the easy availability of firearms as a principal generator of crime. The latter insist that the proper focal point is the offender and that any workable solution lies in the principles of deterrence and appropriate sentencing." This division in Congress, of course, reflects the division in the nation as a whole—one constituency backing the aims of Kennedy-Rodino, and the other those of McClure-Volkmer.

The constituency supporting the Kennedy-Rodino proposal is represented chiefly by the two leading gun-control organizations in America—the National Coalition to Ban Handguns, and Handgun Control, Inc., both with headquarters in Washington. The National Coalition, the smaller of the two, is headed by Michael Beard, a forty-three-year-old former legislative aide. The coalition embraces over thirty religious, labor, political, and civic groups, and its advisory council has included Eugene Carson Blake, John Kenneth Galbraith, Leonard Bernstein, Julian Bond, Robert Drinan, James Farmer, Harvery Cox, Walter Fauntroy, and Norman Lear. Handgun Control, Inc., seeks a limitation on the production and circulation of handguns. The National Coalition goes further, seeking a near-total ban on the production and possession of handguns, whether cheap or expensive, imported or domestically made. Beard told an interviewer in 1981, "We remain convinced that nothing short of an outright ban on civilian possession of handguns will ultimately be effective in reducing handgun crime and saving lives. If you call a total ban extreme, then we're extremist." Therefore, while the National Coalition lobbies strongly against McClure-Volkmer, it isn't as enthusiastic about Kennedy-Rodino as it would be if that bill were also seeking a ban on the production and possession of all handguns, not just the cheap ones. The cheap handgun remains "an easy target for legislators," Beard argues, "because the very name conjures up an image of the proverbial poor, inner-city youth or petty criminal buying one for fifty bucks on a street corner." He maintains that "a larger problem is now posed by the high-quality $200 to $300 handgun purchased by the white, blue-collar homeowner in the suburbs and stashed in a dresser drawer for 'self-protection.'"

"Gun control has been a great liberal cause," a New York City gun buff scoffed some time ago, going on to say that liberals "are not for strict controls, they are just not for any guns at all." Neither part of his statement is strictly true. Though gun regulation *has* been a liberal cause, it has not been a cause for all liberals: there are liberals who want strict controls, and nothing more; there are liberals who want no guns at all; and there are liberals who want no controls at all. There are also gun-control advocates who have nothing liberal in their personal or political backgrounds. One such anomaly is Nelson (Pete) Shields, who leads Handgun Control, Inc. Shields was an executive at E. I. du Pont de Nemours before he joined the anti-gun movement. He had been a Republican all his life, and a devoted hunter as well. And he still has no objections to shotguns. He hates handguns, however: in 1975, his son Nick was killed, on a street in San Francisco, by a member of a gang of gunmen known by the code name Zebra, who were then terrorizing the city. It was after his son's death that Shields took a leave of absence from his job at du Pont and began helping out a small and underfinanced group in Washington called the National Council to Control Handguns. His son's murder, he has explained, "made me wonder if I could do something to stop this from happening to somebody else's kid." In 1978, having retired from du Pont, he became the chairman of the organization, which became Handgun Control, Inc., the following year, and has grown to be the largest organization of its kind in the country. Handgun Control, Inc., now has what it calls a "citizen army" of about a million supporters, about a hundred and seventy-five thousand of whom are members and contribute to its operating budget (two million dollars in 1983). Its national-committee members have included William Ruckelshaus, Edmund G. Brown, Sr., Richard Hatcher, Kenneth Gibson, Martin Luther King, Sr., and John Lindsay. Like the pro-gun movement, Handgun Control, Inc., together with its political-action committee, lobbies in Congress, aids sympathetic groups in local communities, and supports politicians who endorse its objectives and opposes those who oppose them. An example of the last of these activities is a mailing that it sent to New York voters in 1982, which read, in part, "Why . . . is our new Senator, Alfonse D'Amato, co-sponsoring a bill [McClure-Volkmer] to weaken our national law? . . . Why is Senator D'Amato proposing that we begin erasing *every* Federal gun law on the books? . . . Mr. D'Amato has no business sponsoring a bill that endangers the lives of the very people he represents. . . . Why did he do it? Perhaps it's because he received $16,259 from the National Rifle Association's Political Victory Fund in the last election." This and similar letters about other politicians demonstrate how much Handgun Control, Inc., has learned from its powerful N.R.A.-led opposition, which early perfected the use of direct mass mailing to mobilize formidable support for its cause.

The pro-gun lobby—a giant compared to Handgun Control, Inc.—is one of the largest, strongest, and best-financed special-interest groups in the nation's capital. Made up of organizations on the right—the more prominent ones being the Second Amendment Foundation, the Citizens Committee for the Right to Keep and Bear Arms, and the National Rifle Association—it seeks to preserve for its adherents, and for other Americans as well, the right to own and use firearms. It regards all gun-control advocates as "gun-grabbers"—as people whose true objective is not to regulate the possession of firearms but to confiscate all guns. It spreads that belief among its grass-roots following, and scares members of Congress with its ability to organize that belief and translate it into a mass of pro-gun votes.

Though polls show that the pro-gun groups represent a minority opinion in the United States, their membership far outnumbers that of the anti-gun organizations, and they have managed to exercise something resembling a veto over the desire that most Americans have expressed for stronger gun laws. This may be because the opponents of gun control are better organized—and perhaps more organizable—than the proponents. It may also be that they are seldom critical of their leadership, and do not hesitate at election time to put their votes where their gun convictions are. Many gun-control advocates, on the other hand, even those who are organized, do not, as a rule, vote solely on the issue of guns—they won't work to elect or defeat a candidate just because of his position on firearms. So while they continue to hope for stronger gun laws, they help to frustrate their own hopes by maintaining an admirable civic attitude: by continuing to act on the principle that a candidate's stand on a range of national and international issues provides a fairer test of his credentials for office than whether he's likely to support or oppose gun-control measures.

The Second Amendment Foundation and the Citizens Committee for the Right to Keep and Bear Arms are sister organizations. They share an address (in the state of Washington, though the Citizens Committee also has lobbyists on Capitol Hill) and some of the same officers; for instance, Alan Gottlieb, the founder and chairman of the Citizens Committee, is also the president of the Second Amendment Foundation. (His status at the foundation is now in some dispute. Six staff members who were dismissed by Gottlieb are in turn seeking his removal for alleged financial irregularities.) The Citizens Committee is the larger and more politically active of the two, and its advisory council includes well over a hundred United States senators and representatives—a sign of its influence in Congress. Though the Citizens Committee isn't the major force in the gun lobby, it's a formidable one. Since its founding in 1971, it has grown from nine thousand members to more than five hundred thousand. Each year, it spends more than a million dollars lobbying in Congress and state legislatures, and on numerous "action projects"—all with the stated aim of preserving "our *right* to keep and bear arms."

The National Rifle Association, thanks to the size of its membership, the size of its treasury, and the power of its clout in Congress, is the undisputed champion of the pro-gun lobby. It has a membership of about three million, and in 1983 its treasury financed a budget of fifty-two million dollars, compared with two million dollars spent that year by the much smaller Handgun Control, Inc. A 1983 issue of the N.R.A.'s *Reports from Washington* said, "The National Rifle Association spent more money communicating with association members during the 1981–82 election year than did any other organization in America, according to figures released . . . by the Federal Election Commission. The F.E.C. examinations . . . show the N.R.A. spent $803,656 on literature and other types of information designed to acquaint . . . members with the policies of various candidates in the federal election races. . . . One group not listed in the report was Handgun Control, Inc. . . . But H.C.I.'s PAC gave more than $50,000 directly to candidates with pro-gun-control sentiments, according to F.E.C. documents."

Like Pete Shields, of Handgun Control, Inc., Harlon Carter, the head of the N.R.A., has had a life marked by the tragedy of gunfire. Carter took over the N.R.A. leadership decades after he was convicted of shooting and killing a Mexican-American in Texas, his native state. The incident occurred in 1931, when Carter and the victim were teen-agers, and it gained no wide attention until 1981, when—Carter having become a luminary of the pro-gun movement—the Laredo *Times* dug up the story from its files and reprinted it. According to that report, Carter was convicted of murder and sentenced to three years in jail, but his conviction was overturned when the state Court of Appeals ruled that some witnesses were untrustworthy, and the charges against him were later dropped. In 1982, while the N.R.A. was holding its annual meeting in Philadelphia, the Philadelphia *Inquirer* also ran the old story of the shooting incident. But if it was news to the assembly of N.R.A. members it did nothing to alter the high esteem in which they held their leader. Nor did it moderate Carter's militant rhetoric on behalf of the right to own and use guns. "We can reasonably and rightfully . . . aspire to a time when few politicians, mindful of their futures, will oppose us," he told the group. "Don't trust the politician who won't trust you with a gun."

If one of the original members of the N.R.A. had risen to make such statements at a meeting, he might have been asked to take himself and his views to a more appropriate organization. The N.R.A. was anything but a gun lobby when it came into being, in 1871. For decades after its founding—in New York City—its main and almost sole purpose was the teaching of long-range marksmanship to the post–Civil War generation of riflemen. In the early years of this century, having moved its headquarters to Washington, D.C., it became an organization for hunters, farmers, ranchers, sports shooters, and gun collectors, and a sponsor of rifle clubs and target-shooting contests around the nation. This essentially sporting and practical group of gun fanciers became politicized, and radically so, during the sixties, when political assassinations and race riots and the proliferation of crimes involving guns reawoke public anxiety over the destructiveness of firearms in American life. That anxiety was one of the main forces behind the passage of the 1968 Gun Control Act, and the act's passage hastened the transformation of the N.R.A. into a militant advocate and defender of gun-owning rights.

Since then, the N.R.A. has led the fight against almost all attempts to pass stricter gun laws. In the 1980 campaign, it not only took the unprecedented steps of endorsing a candidate for President and claiming credit for many of the votes that put him in the White House but also, through its Political Victory Fund, spent more than a million dollars to help elect other pro-gun candidates. The conservative landslide to which N.R.A. contributed strengthened its position not only in the White House but in Congress as well. Drawing inspiration and justification from the Second Amendment to the Constitution, it views as sacrosanct the civilian right to own and use guns. Further, it sees the exercise of that right as a potential defense against any repressive or authoritarian government that might one day arise in the United States. That is the point the N.R.A. was making in full-page newspaper ads it ran after Lech Walesa and the Solidarity movement had been crushed. "The actions of the Polish Government in suspending basic rights and liberties of its citizens should cause every American to say a silent thank you for the foresight of the drafters of the U.S. Constitution," the ad proclaimed. "Poland has precisely the firearms laws that the N.R.A. has been opposing in the United States. . . . And so long as the Second Amendment is not infringed what is happening in Poland can never happen in these United States."

"The Right to Keep and Bear Arms" is only one of a number of slogans by which the N.R.A. and its allies make their case against gun-control legislation. Others, proclaimed on bumper stickers across the nation, are "Gun Laws Don't Work," "If Guns Are Outlawed Only Outlaws Will Have Guns," "Registration Is the First Step to Confiscation," and, of course, "Guns Don't Kill, People Do." These slogans are also the basis of pamphlets, letters to the faithful, newspaper ads, speeches, and articles in the gun press, and of Alan Gottlieb's book *The Rights of Gun Owners*—a manifesto of the pro-gun movement. Gottlieb has told an interviewer, "For over a decade, law-abiding Americans who own and use guns for legitimate purposes have been blamed by political hacks and extreme leftist media ideologues for the rising rates of crime in our country when the real cause for these rates is the permissive, mealy-mouthed, mollycoddling attitude of these same hacks and ideologues." In "Anti-Gunners Are a Threat to America!," an article published in a 1982 issue of *Guns & Ammo*, the writer Bill Clede maintains, "Pro-gunners are in favor of gun control. They want mandatory sentences for those using firearms in crime. They want to eliminate plea bargaining of gun charges against criminals. They do *not* favor proposed laws that harass the honest citizen while having no effect on crime. . . . So, if the anti-gunners win, we 'the people' have no right to peaceably assemble, maintain personal security, retain rights not delegated [to] the federal government, or to keep and bear arms. . . . As far as I am concerned, the greatest threat of all this furor over 'gun control' has nothing to do with guns. It is a threat to my country and the democratic principles I believe in."

Gun-control advocates, for their part, wonder why the pro-gun lobbyists resist so strenuously almost every attempt to regulate the manufacture, circulation, possession, and use of handguns. Why, since nobody is trying to regulate long guns, does the pro-gun lobby oppose the slightest restriction on the production and use of snubbies—the weapons that account for so many of the murders and other crimes involving guns in the United States? In 1981, the Most Reverend James Hickey, the Archbishop of Washington, D.C., was denounced by the Citizens Committee for the Right to Keep and Bear Arms as a member of the "gun-grabbing" clergy, for having said that he dearly wished to see "the elimination of handguns from society." What could have been so reprehensible about the Archbishop's wish? One answer may be found in something that Alan Gottlieb has said against the movement to ban cheap handguns: "One compelling argument against such a ban has been brought forward by Ernest van de Haag. He reasons that both the poor and the elderly are the chief victims of crime and cannot necessarily afford expensive handguns for self-defense, and since inner-city police protection is so poor, many citizens must rely on self-protection." . . .

HANDGUN CONTROL[2]

The Problem

Crimes committed by individuals using handguns represent a serious problem of violence in our nation. (1981 Attorney General's Task Force on Violent Crime)

[2]Excerpt from a pamphlet published by Handgun Control, Inc. Reprinted by permission.

Handguns in the wrong hands take the lives of more than 20,000 Americans every year in homicides, accidents, and suicides. Each year, handguns are used to wound, rob, rape or threaten hundreds of thousands more.

Some violent tragedies have moved Americans to action. New laws are starting to crack down on drunk driving, for example. Yet Congress has done little to keep handguns from falling into the wrong hands: the hands of minors, criminals, drunks, drug users, and the mentally incompetent.

The U.S. is the only nation in the world which allows such shocking crime and violence to continue. We are the only industrialized nation in the world which places few effective restrictions on handgun availability. Foreign experience demonstrates that handgun laws work. In fact, in 1983, the latest year for which statistics are available, handguns were used to murder: **35 people in Japan, 8 in Great Britain, 6 in Canada, 10 in Australia, 7 in Sweden, 27 in Switzerland, . . . and 9,014 in the United States.**

The Obstacle

. . . the meanest, most unforgiving lobby in the land. (The Miami *Herald*)

For more than half a century, public opinion polls have demonstrated that the vast majority of Americans want tougher laws to keep handguns out of the wrong hands. For example, a 1981 Gallup Poll found that 91% of Americans support a waiting period and background check for handgun purchasers.

Despite the polls, Congress has refused to act. Standing in the way is the largest single-issue lobby in the nation—the National Rifle Association (NRA). The NRA, with its nearly three million members, not only blocks new law, but is systematically working for repeal of existing law. Incredibly, the NRA even fights to allow the sale of plastic handguns, cop-killer bullets and machine guns. With an annual budget of $60 million, the NRA has the money, the numbers, and the clout to influence and intimidate the Congress.

Handgun Control Incorporated

. . . the chief lobby on the topic . . . (The New York *Times*)
. . . the country's leading anti-gun lobby . . . (*Congressional Quarterly*)

Handgun Control, Inc., is a non-profit, citizens organization working for passage of federal legislation to keep handguns out of the wrong hands. Handgun Control was founded in 1974 by Dr. Mark Borinsky, who as a student was held up by two men with handguns. When Borinsky came to Washington, D.C., he attempted to join a handgun control organization. Surprised that none existed, Borinsky founded the National Council to Control Handguns (NCCH).

Later that year, Borinsky was joined by N. T. "Pete" Shields, a DuPont executive whose son, Nick, was murdered with a handgun during the 1974 Zebra killings in San Francisco. In 1975, Shields left DuPont to become executive director of NCCH, and was later elected Chairman.

By 1980, NCCH, renamed Handgun Control, Inc., counted 80,000 supporters. Prompted by the shootings of John Lennon and Ronald Reagan, hundreds of thousands of Americans came forward to join Handgun Control's battle.

Since then, Handgun Control's focus has been on recruiting the numbers of supporters necessary to win passage of effective handgun law. Now, more than *one million* Americans have joined Handgun Control's campaign to keep handguns out of the wrong hands. We represent a broad coalition of concerned Americans including law enforcement officials, victims of handgun violence, Hollywood celebrities, police on the beat, and others who want to help prevent handgun violence.

The Legislative Goal

. . . The International Association of Chiefs of Police urges the law enforcement community within each state to support and encourage the enactment of legislation pertinent to the screening of handgun purchasers . . . (The International Association of Chiefs of Police, 1981 Resolution)

Handgun Control seeks to pass federal legislation to keep handguns out of the wrong hands. Our legislative agenda includes provisions which police and other law enforcement experts have demanded for years:

• **a waiting period and background check** to screen out illegal handgun purchasers such as convicted felons and drug users.

• **a mandatory jail sentence** for using a handgun in the commission of a crime.

• **a license-to-carry law,** requiring a special license to carry a handgun outside one's home or place of business.

• **a ban on the manufacture and sale of snub-nosed handguns;** the Saturday Night Specials used in two-thirds of handgun crime.

• **restriction on the sale of UZI-type assault weapons,** the weapons of war like that used in the 1983 McDonald's massacre in California.

• **a ban on the manufacture and sale of plastic handguns** which make metal detectors and airport screening devices useless.

A Decade of Achievement

(ON THE McCLURE-VOLKMER BILL:) Due in large part to the professionalism and effective advocacy of HCI, we were able to develop and agree upon a number of amendments which significantly improved the bill. (Senator Robert Dole [R–Kansas])

(ON COP-KILLER BULLETS:) . . . It is extremely unlikely that the efforts of the single-issue group on the other side of this issue—the NRA—would have been overcome except for Handgun Control, Inc., and the police organizations. (The Baltimore *Sun*)

In its short life, Handgun Control has grown from one handgun victim's vision to an organization *one million strong*. We are Americans from all walks of life who want to put an end to the senseless brutality of handgun violence. Our record of progress includes:

• For seven years, the NRA attempted to pass legislation to dismantle the 1968 Gun Control Act, our nation's federal gun law. The bill included provisions to allow mail-order gun sales and interstate handgun sales. When this NRA-backed bill passed in 1986, Handgun Control and the nation's police succeeded in gutting the bill by removing most of its damaging provisions. In the final analysis, little harm was done to our nation's handgun law. In fact, the '68 law was strengthened.

Handgun Control helped convince Congress to ban the sale of machine guns and the kits used to convert other firearms into these deadly automatic weapons. A provision to stop the importation of parts of Saturday Night Specials was also enacted.

• Despite strong opposition and heavy lobbying by the National Rifle Association, Handgun Control and the nation's police persuaded the Congress to pass a bill banning armor-piercing, "cop-killer" bullets.

• Working with citizens and state and local legislatures, Handgun Control has helped many jurisdictions pass stronger handgun laws. We successfully defended the Washington, D.C. handgun law in the courts. We assisted citizens of Washington state, Connecticut, and Hawaii in passage of comprehensive state-wide laws. We also assisted the Village of Morton Grove in the legal defense of its historic handgun ordinance.

• Handgun Control was the first organization to establish a handgun control political action committee. The Handgun Control PAC provides financial support to candidates seeking federal office and supports incumbents who work for passage of laws to keep handguns out of the wrong hands. Despite NRA PAC expenditures in excess of three million dollars, our PAC maintained an 85–95% success rate in the 1984 and 1986 national elections.

• Handgun Control sued under the Freedom of Information Act to obtain data on U.S. handgun production, making available, for the first time, comprehensive information on the secretive American handgun industry.

From One Million Strong
to Five Million Strong

To overcome the power of the National Rifle Association, Handgun Control must expand its support base from **one million strong** to **five million strong.** Our task is to recruit the numbers necessary to win this fight, organize these supporters, and apply strong pressure on the Congress.

Handgun Control works to get *you* involved. We provide supporters with the information they need to bring the handgun control message to their legislators. Through alerts to targeted Congressional districts, we mobilize our supporters into a grass-roots lobbying force. Handgun Control supporters write, call, and visit their legislators, providing vital local lobbying power.

Here's how Handgun Control works to represent you:

LOBBYING

Handgun Control works closely with Members of Congress on Capitol Hill to promote legislation which will prevent handgun violence. We are your voice, and our staff works to represent the views of millions of Americans who want to end handgun violence. Handgun Control provides expert witnesses for testimony on the handgun issue in Senate and House hearings. We work with legislators in drafting effective legislation.

COMMUNICATIONS

Handgun Control works to keep the handgun issue before the public. Our staff makes appearances on television and radio programs and promotes handgun control through a comprehensive media relations program. We produce and assemble research on the effectiveness of handgun laws both in the U.S. and abroad. Handgun Control also provides research materials for students, academicians, and the general public.

GRASSROOTS NETWORK

Handgun Control maintains a national Network of grassroots activists who are working to recruit new supporters and educate Americans on the issue of handgun violence. Networkers are organized by Congressional district and form the core of our grassroots lobbying effort. Individuals participate in a wide variety of projects including recruiting members, providing speakers for schools and civic clubs, testifying before state and local legislative bodies, appearing on television and radio, and communicating with their Senators and Representatives.

POLITICAL ACTION

Handgun Control provides financial contributions to candidates for federal office who support laws to keep handguns out of the wrong hands. The PAC distributes questionnaires to candidates and assembles information on their positions on the handgun issue.

HANDGUN FACTS: TWELVE QUESTIONS
AND ANSWERS ABOUT HANDGUN CONTROL[3]

1. What is Handgun Control, Inc.?

Handgun Control is a non-profit citizens organization working to pass federal law to keep handguns out of the wrong hands. Such legislation would include: a waiting period and background check for handgun purchasers; a ban on the further production and sale of Saturday Night Specials; mandatory sentences for using a gun in a crime; mandatory handgun safety-training programs for handgun purchasers; and tighter requirements for handgun dealers and manufacturers.

2. Do we really need a new national law to keep handguns out of the wrong hands?

Yes. Current state handgun laws make up a patchwork of varying strengths. These laws are easily undermined by individuals who buy and sell handguns across state lines. For example, in New York, more than 90% of handguns used in crime are purchased out of state. Clearly, criminals have great difficulty obtaining handguns in New York. But because of weaker laws in other states, the channels through which criminals obtain their handguns are wide open. A uniform federal law to keep handguns out of the wrong hands will close off the criminal's easy access to handguns.

3. Isn't it true that "guns don't kill people—people do?"

People do kill people, but they do so mostly with handguns. In fact, handguns are used 2½ times more often than any other murder weapon. Automobiles are also dangerous, therefore we require driver licensing and automobile registration. We should require similar precautions for deadly handguns.

4. What will a waiting period and background check accomplish?

A waiting period with a background check serves two purposes. First, it will serve as a cooling-off period for those who would buy

[3]Reprint of pamphlet by Handgun Control, Inc. Reprinted by permission.

handguns in a moment of desperation to use in a suicide or a "crime of passion." In addition, a criminal records check will screen out purchasers who, under law, are prohibited from handgun ownership. A comprehensive approach will help reduce accidents, suicides, and murders. According to a 1981 Gallup Poll, a waiting period is favored by 91% of the American people. For years, national police organizations have called for this measure.

5. How will handgun control help reduce accidents?

Through mandatory safety training courses, handgun owners can learn the proper way to store and maintain their handguns, thus reducing the likelihood that these weapons will be stolen or fall into the hands of children and result in a tragic accident.

6. What is a Saturday Night Special and why should it be banned?

According to studies by Cox Newspapers, the Bureau of Alcohol, Tobacco and Firearms, and Florida Technological University, criminals prefer handguns with a barrel length of 3 inches or less. These easily concealed handguns (known as snub-nosed handguns, snubbies, or Saturday Night Specials) are the weapon of choice among criminals and assassins. Nearly ⅔ of handgun rapes, robberies and muggings involve a Saturday Night Special. Criminals do not use longer-barreled weapons because they prefer the concealability of the snubbie. According to Florida Technological University, nearly 70% of convicted felons admit using Saturday Night Specials. Criminals need the concealability the snubbie affords; the homeowner does not.

7. Why doesn't Handgun Control concern itself simply with punishing criminals?

HCI does support mandatory sentencing for using a gun in a crime. A mandatory sentence of 2–10 years for a first offense and 5–25 for subsequent offenses would help keep gun-wielding criminals off the streets. But we also believe in preventive medicine. By making it more difficult for criminals, drug addicts, etc., to get handguns, and by ensuring that law-abiding citizens know how to maintain their handguns, we can reduce handgun violence.

8. In Switzerland, everyone is required to own a gun and yet the murder rate is very low. Why?

In Switzerland, all men are members of the militia and are issued rifles and ammunition by the government. These long guns are registered and all ammunition must be accounted for. Handguns are even more tightly controlled. Swiss law requires a background check, a permit to possess a handgun, and handgun registration.

9. Doesn't the Second Amendment to the Constitution make handgun control unconstitutional?

In its entirety, the Second Amendment reads: "A well-regulated Militia, being necessary to the security of a free State, the right of the people to keep and bear arms shall not be infringed."

The U.S. Supreme Court has interpreted this amendment on five separate occasions. In addition, nearly forty lower court decisions have addressed the amendment. All have ruled that the second amendment guarantees a state's right to maintain a militia.

Most recently, on October 3, 1983, the Supreme Court refused to overturn a handgun law in Morton Grove, Illinois. The Supreme Court let stand a Court of Appeals ruling which stated, ". . . possession of handguns by individuals is not part of the right to keep and bear arms. . . ."

10. What about the argument that when guns are outlawed, only outlaws will have guns?

Under any realistic federal handgun law, handguns will still be available to responsible citizens. Rifles and shotguns will not be affected at all. Handgun laws will simply make it easier to keep these weapons out of the hands of felons, fugitives, drug addicts, mental incompetents, and children.

11. Where has handgun control ever worked in the U.S.?

A study of the Bartley-Fox law in Massachusetts, which requires a mandatory jail sentence for carrying a handgun outside one's home or place of business without a license, was conducted by the Center for Applied Social Research at Northeastern University. The authors concluded that there has been a significant decrease in handgun murders, assaults and robberies since the law was enacted in 1974. Handgun murders have dropped nearly 50%; armed robberies more than 35%. Boston, once ranked 8th for murder in the U.S., now ranks 19th, according to the F.B.I. Uniform Crime Reports.

In South Carolina, after tightening requirements for handgun purchases, the murder rate dropped 28%. Washington, D.C., has seen a 30% reduction in handgun death since passage of a 1977 handgun law.

Police officials in Columbus, Georgia, say the city's 3-day waiting period and background check are extremely effective. According to the Columbus Police Chief, "We catch two a week with felony convictions [trying to buy handguns]." And the California Attorney General's Office reports that the state's 15-day waiting period and background check screened out some 1,200 prohibited handgun buyers in 1981 alone.

12. Where do the nation's police stand on the handgun issue?
For years, our nation's law enforcement experts have called for tougher measures to keep handguns out of the wrong hands. The International Association of Chiefs of Police, the largest police leadership organization in the nation, has stated:

We believe the following provisions must be incorporated [into the law]:
• **a waiting or cooling off period**
• **positive verification of the identity of a prospective purchaser or permit applicant**
• **mandatory fingerprint/criminal record check at the state and federal level of all applicants by local police agencies**
• **the issuance of a photograph identification card to approved handgun purchasers**
• **mandatory sentencing of persons convicted of crime involving a handgun**

TEN MYTHS ABOUT "GUN CONTROL"[4]

The only way to discourage the gun culture is to remove the guns from the hands and shoulders of people who are not in the law enforcement business. (The New York *Times*, September 24, 1975)

That editorial conclusion by the nation's most influential news journal, one noted for its advocacy of individual liberties, represents the absolute extreme in the firearms controversy—

[4]Reprint of a pamphlet by the National Rifle Association. Reprinted by permission.

that no citizen can be trusted to own any kind of firearm. This expressed attitude is particularly ironic since the overwhelming majority of the 60 million American firearms owners have done nothing to deserve such a sweeping condemnation. It is the product of a series of myths which—through incessant repetition—has been mistaken for truth. These myths are being exploited to generate fear and mistrust of the decent and responsible Americans who own firearms. Yet, as this brochure proves, none of these myths will stand up under the cold light of fact.

> *MYTH: "The majority of Americans favor strict new additional Federal gun controls."*

Until the fall of 1975, when Decision Making Information (DMI), a public opinion research firm of Santa Ana, California, completed a comprehensive survey of Americans' thinking on firearms control, virtually no in-depth public opinion research on the subject existed. That first effort showed indisputably that the American people strongly support the rights of private firearms ownership.

The second and most recent DMI poll, released in March 1979, reaffirms these early results. The DMI project, directed by Dr. Richard B. Wirthlin, was based on a scientifically selected sample of registered voters in 1,500 in-home interviews in May and June of 1978 and supported by in-depth telephone interviews of 1,010 registered voters in December.

Among these findings:

• 88 percent of registered voters believe they have an individual right to keep and bear arms.

• Gun ownership was acknowledged in 47 percent of voters' households, with 23 percent of the total sample having one or more handguns in the home. In 14 percent of all voters' households, or 13 million households, a gun had been used in defense of self, family or property. With many voters having a direct experience with firearms for self-defense, DMI finds that 83 percent feel "most people who have guns in their homes feel safer because of them."

• Crime is perceived as a serious problem for the 1980s with the most feared crimes being crimes of violence committed by criminals, especially murder in the course of another crime and robbery/mugging. So-called "crimes of passion"—murder by a relative or friend—are of little concern, ranking with "white collar crimes" of fraud/embezzlement/forgery.

• 93 percent favor strict mandatory penalties for criminal misuse of firearms in commission of crime. According to DMI, "The electorate clearly sees steps to increase or hasten the punishment suffered by criminals, especially violent criminals, as the best way to fight crime."

• In an open-ended question on the best means to fight crime, only one percent suggests gun controls. DMI says that "'gun control' . . . does not spontaneously occur to voters as an anti-crime measure."

• 83 percent oppose a ban on handguns. 72 percent believe that domestic shootings do not justify a handgun ban. Over 80 percent reject the arguments that banning handguns would prevent assassination attempts on public officials.

• 88 percent agree that "registration of handguns will not prevent criminals from acquiring or using them for illegal purposes," and 61 percent oppose the federal government's spending massive sums for a registration system. Furthermore, DMI finds that, "71 percent would be concerned about the loss of privacy entailed in computerized files virtually inherent in a nationwide registration system."

• 51 percent feel that national gun registration might well lead to confiscation.

The general consensus of the DMI survey finds that while most Americans see crime as worsening, they do not view gun restrictions as effective measures for government to institute in fighting crime. Above all else, the DMI findings conclude that, "Clearly, a majority of the American people want government to focus on tougher treatment of criminals before trying new social engineering as the treatment for crime."

These findings are supported by the findings of a Caddell poll (Cambridge Reports, Inc.) sponsored by Milton Eisenhower's Center for the Study and Prevention of Handgun Violence in 1978. Although that Center is on record favoring restrictive gun laws and the poll's question order and wording reflected this bias, the poll confirmed overwhelming opposition to a handgun ban and found that 78 percent of the American people believe that, "Gun control laws affect only law-abiding citizens; criminals will always be able to find guns."

Without a doubt, the truest test of public attitude on "gun control" comes when the electorate has a chance to speak on the issue.

In November 1976, Massachusetts voters faced a referendum question calling for a ban on all handguns. That statewide ban-the-handgun question was crushed by a margin of more than 2-to-1. During the 1980s, voters of New Hampshire, Nevada, North Dakota, and West Virginia adopted, by overwhelming percentages, constitutional amendments guaranteeing the right of citizens to keep and bear arms.

And, in November 1982, Californians rejected, by a 63–37 percent margin, a statewide handgun initiative that called for the registration of all handguns and a "freeze" on the number of handguns allowed in the state.

That initiative was also opposed by the majority of California's law enforcement community. Fifty-one of the state's 58 working sheriffs opposed Proposition 15, as did 101 Chiefs of Police. Rank and file lawmen, voting through their respective associations, voiced their opposition. Nine law enforcement organizations went on record against the initiative.

In 1985, in the midst of the Congressional debate over the McClure-Volkmer Firearms Owners' Protection Act, the American Federation of Police surveyed its 50,000 members and found that 96% supported the right of the people to have handguns for protection, 96% rejected the notion that a handgun ban would disarm criminals, and 94% supported, instead, additional penalties for criminals who use guns to commit crimes.

And when the NRA and United Sportsmen of Florida sought legislation to ease the state's carry-for-protection law and to pre-empt local anti-gun ordinances, they were joined by the five leading police organizations in the state.

MYTH: *"Since a gun in a home is six times more likely to kill a family member than to stop a criminal, armed citizens are not a deterrent to crime."*

This myth, stemming from a superficial "study" of firearm accidents in the Cleveland, Ohio, area, merely represents a comparison of 148 accidental deaths (and some suicides) to the deaths of 23 intruders killed by homeowners over a 16-year period.

Gross errors in the "study" and in its citation by "gun control" advocates include: no distinction is made between handgun and long gun deaths; all accidental firearm fatalities were counted whether the deceased was part of the "family" or not; all accidents were counted whether they occurred in the home or not, while self-defense outside the home was excluded; almost half the self-defense uses of guns in the home were excluded on the grounds that the criminal intruder killed was not a total stranger to the home defender; and Cleveland's experience with crime and accidents during those years was atypical of the nation as a whole—and, indeed, of Cleveland since the mid-1970s.

Moreover, in a later study, the same researchers noted that roughly 10 percent of killings by civilians are justifiable homicides.

Gun ownership by law-abiding citizens averts crime.

Research by Professors James Wright and Peter Rossi, based on a landmark study funded by the Department of Justice, points to the armed citizen or the threat of the armed citizen as possibly the most effective deterrent to crime and the nation.

Wright and Rossi questioned over 1,800 prisoners serving time in prisons across the nation and found:

• 85 percent agreed that the "smart criminal" will attempt to find out if a potential victim is armed.

• 75 percent felt that burglars avoided occupied dwellings for fear of being shot.

• 80 percent of "handgun predators" had encountered armed citizens.

• 53 percent did not commit a specific crime for fear that the victim was armed.

• 57 percent of "handgun predators" were scared off or shot at by armed victims.

• 60 percent felt that the typical criminal feared being shot by citizens more than he feared being shot by police.

Professor Gary Kleck of Florida State University estimates that 1,500–2,800 felons are legally killed annually in "excusable self-defense" or "justifiable" shootings by civilians, and 8–16,000 criminals are wounded. This compares to 300–600 justifiable killings by police.

Yet, in most instances, civilians used a firearm to threaten, apprehend or shoot at a criminal, or to fire a warning shot without injuring anyone.

Based on surveys commissioned by handgun-ban advocates (Caddell, Peter Hart Associates), Kleck estimates that annually nearly 650,000 Americans use handguns for protection from criminals—with over 300,000 additional protective uses of long guns. U.S. Department of Justice victimization surveys show that protective use of a gun lessens the chance that robberies, rapes, and assaults will be successfully completed while reducing the likelihood of victim injury. Clearly, criminals fear armed citizens.

MYTH: "The only purpose of a handgun is to kill people."

This often repeated statement is patently untrue, but to those Americans whose only knowledge of firearms is the nightly carnage and bloody violence of television, it might seem believable. But when anti-gun scholar James Wright of the University of Massachusetts read some sportsmen's publications, he reached a different conclusion: "Even the most casual and passing familiarity with this literature is therefore sufficient to belie the contention that handguns have 'no legitimate sport or recreational use.'"

There are an estimated 50 to 60 million privately-owned handguns in the United States. They are used for hunting, target shooting, protection of families and businesses and numerous other legitimate and lawful purposes. Only an infinitesimal percent are ever used by criminals in criminal conduct. In 1986, for example, the FBI reported fewer than 8,000 homicides in which handguns were used. That amounts to less than .01 percent (one hundredth of one percent) of the privately owned handguns being used to kill. That fact alone renders the myth about the "only purpose" of handguns absurd, for more than 99 percent of all handguns are used neither to murder nor for any other criminal purpose.

But why do so many Americans wish to own handguns? Approximately 1.5 million people hunt with handguns each year. Still more people target shoot either in formal competition or as a weekend hobby. Millions of Americans are collectors who appreciate handguns for design, workmanship or historic qualities.

But by far the most commonly cited reason for owning a handgun is self-defense. At least one sixth of the families in America own handguns for protection and security.

The purpose of a handgun in the home is to preserve life and to discourage acts of violence. It is the immediate means a family has to thwart ultimate criminal force. A handgun's function is one of insurance as well as defense. A handgun in the home is a contingency, based on the knowledge that if there ever comes a time when it is needed, no substitute will do. Certainly no violent intent is implied, any more than a purchaser of life insurance intends to die soon.

Indeed, in a survey of prisoners, Professor James Wright of the University of Massachusetts found:

• 88 percent agreed that "a criminal who wants a handgun is going to get one, no matter how much it costs."

• 82 percent felt that "gun laws only affect law-abiding citizens; criminals will always be able to get guns."

Even the National Coalition to Ban Handguns (NCBH) has said that "criminals do not leave their guns behind to be traced, nor would they register them in the first place." And registration is almost never useful in tracing a gun—unless the person who has misused the gun is already in custody, in which case tracing the gun is meaningless.

Further, felons are constitutionally exempt from the registration requirement. According to a U.S. Supreme Court decision, since a felon cannot possess a firearm, forcing him to register a firearm would violate the Fifth Amendment provision against self-incrimination. So, only law-abiding citizens would be required to comply with registration.

MYTH: "Most murders are argument-related 'crimes of passion' against a relative, neighbor, friend or acquaintance, committed by previously law-abiding individuals with no prior criminal records."

In fact, the vast majority of murders are committed by persons with long-established patterns of violent criminal behavior. According to analyses by the Senate Subcommittee on Juvenile Delinquency, by the FBI, and the Chicago, New York City, and other police departments, about 70 percent of suspected murderers have criminal careers of long standing—as do nearly half their victims.

And FBI data showing that roughly 55 percent of the murderers were known to their victims is not so surprising. Recent studies by the Justice Department suggest that persons who live violent lives exhibit those violent tendencies "both within their home and among their family and friends and outside their home among strangers in society."

A complete Lie.

In addition, circumstances which might suggest "crimes of passion" or "spontaneous" arguments, such as a lover's triangle, arguments over money or property, and alcohol-related brawls, comprise less than 10 percent of criminal homicides.

Further, numerous studies debunk the "crime of passion" myth. For example, a recent National Institute of Justice study reveals that the victims of family violence often suffer repeated problems from the same person for months or even years, and if not successfully resolved, such incidents can eventually result in serious injury or death. Indeed, studies conducted by the Police Foundation show that at least 90 percent of all homicides, by whatever means committed, involving family members, had been preceded by some other violent incident serious enough that police were summoned.

Professor James Wright describes the typical incident of family violence as "that mythical crime of passion" and denies that it is an isolated incident by otherwise normally placid and loving individuals. The available research shows that it is in fact "the culminating event in a long history of inter-personal violence between the parties," Wright says.

Further, Wright notes that handguns do not play the aggressive role most often attributed to them.

"The common pattern, the more common pattern, is for wives to shoot their husbands. Proportionately, men kill their women by other means, more brutal means, more degrading means. To deny that woman the right to own the firearm is in some sense to guarantee in perpetuity to her husband the right to beat her at will," says Wright.

MYTH: *"Stiff gun control laws work as evidenced by the low crime rates in England and Japan."*

All criminologists studying the firearms issue reject simple comparisons of violent crime among foreign countries as meaningless. It is impossible to draw valid conclusions without taking into account differences in the collection of crime data, and the political, cultural, racial, religious, and economic disparities among countries. Such factors are not only hard to compare, they are rarely, if ever, taken into account.

Only one scholar, attorney David Kopel, has attempted to evaluate the impact of "gun control" on crime in several foreign countries, and he concluded: "Despite the claims of the American gun control movement, gun control does not deserve credit for the low crime rates in Britain, Japan, or other nations." He noted that Israel and Switzerland, with more widespread firearms ownership than in the U.S., had crime rates comparable to or lower than the usual foreign examples. And he stated: "Foreign style gun control is doomed to failure in America; not only does it depend on search and seizure too intrusive for American standards, it postulates an authoritarian philosophy of government fundamentally at odds with the individualist, egalitarian . . . American ethos."

Foreign countries are two to six times more effective in solving crimes and punishing criminals than America. Revolving-door justice is the problem. In London, about 20% of reported robberies end in conviction; in New York City, less than 5% result in conviction, and in those cases imprisonment is frequently not imposed. Nonetheless, England annually has twice as many homicides with firearms as before adopting its tough laws. During the past dozen years (1974–1986), the handgun-related robbery rate rose over 700% in Britain, compared to a 17% drop in the U.S.

Part of Japan's low crime rate can be explained by the sheer efficiency of its criminal justice system—an efficiency aided by having fewer protections of the right to privacy than exist in the United States. The most basic reason, however, is the widespread respect for law and order so deeply ingrained in the Japanese citizenry. This cultural factor has been passed along to their descendants in the United States, and the murder rate for Japanese Americans—who have access to firearms—is even lower than the murder rate in Japan itself.

The "availability" of firearms has no relationship to crime. If gun availability were a factor in crime rates, the world's highest crime rate would be in Switzerland where every able-bodied man between the ages of 18 and 60 has a machine gun and ammunition readily available in his home. Yet Switzerland has a lower crime rate than either Japan or England where private ownership of firearms is virtually prohibited.

MYTH: *"Law abiding citizens have no reason to fear licensing and registration laws."*

In 1982, Chicago enacted a "handgun freeze" and registration law. In explaining why most residents have not complied with the law, one city councilman explained: "These people fear home invasions. They worry about their safety." And he said that citizens will continue to refuse to register their guns out of fear the firearms will someday be confiscated. Indeed, letters were sent by the Chicago Police Department instructing gun owners who had not registered their firearms to surrender them to the nearest police station within three days.

In 1976, firearms prohibitionists in Massachusetts intended to use existing handgun owner licensing lists in an effort to confiscate all legally owned handguns in that state if a proposed ban initiative passed. Massachusetts voters, in rejecting the handgun ban referendum by a 2-to-1 margin, confirmed that "law-abiding citizens have every reason to fear licensing and registration laws."

As stated by Charles Morgan, avowed handgun prohibitionist and director of the American Civil Liberties Union's (ACLU) Washington office, in an October 1, 1975, hearing of the House Subcommittee on Crime: "I have not one doubt, even if I am in agreement with the National Rifle Association, that that kind of a record-keeping procedure is the first to step to eventual confiscation under one administration or another."

In 1975, the Cleveland City Council enacted a ban on the so-called "Saturday Night Special," which was later challenged and held unconstitutional in Municipal Court. In 1976, the Council enacted a handgun registration ordinance and, dutifully, firearms owners obeyed. Subsequently, when an appeals court reversed the earlier Municipal Court decision and reinstated the "SNS" ban, all of those registered firearms were declared illegal contraband and subject to confiscation. Police notified gun owners about the changed ruling using gun registration lists.

The local reaction to the quick change from registration to confiscation forced the police to postpone the confiscation. But the threat was very real.

Given these threats, it is hardly surprising that surveys consistently indicate that only about 25% compliance can be expected to a registration/licensing law.

While the supposed objective of registration laws is to keep guns out of the hands of criminals, common sense says that the criminal won't register his gun. Thus, it is the law-abiding citizens who will be made to pay the price for such schemes.

Total registration would establish a large bureaucracy at considerable expense to the taxpayer. Based on reports by the Comptroller General of the United States and the Office of the Attorney General of the State of California, the cost of handgun registration and verification of handgun transfers would be somewhere in the neighborhood of $12 to $50 per gun registered or transferred.

Additional costs would be incurred by diverting police from dealing with crime to investigating and processing paperwork on law-abiding citizens. Indirect costs to a national registration system would include increased crime, as well as a federally mandated increase in the size, hence the cost, of state and local police departments.

Finally, a registration/licensing requirement would invade people's privacy by creating a massive government data bank second only to the Social Security System. According to the national legal director of the American Civil Liberties Union, any such system could be abused as an invasion of privacy because, "once you establish a data bank for one purpose it almost invariably gets used for more."

MYTH: "The right guaranteed under the Second Amendment is limited specifically to the arming of a 'well-regulated Militia' that can be compared today to the National Guard."

The Second Amendment reads: "A well-regulated Militia, being necessary to the security of a free State, the right of the people to keep and bear Arms, shall not be infringed."

In contrast to other portions of the Constitution, this Amendment contains no qualifiers, no "buts," or "excepts." It is a straightforward statement affirming the people's right to possess firearms.

The perception that the Second Amendment guarantees a collective rather than an individual right is totally inaccurate. The term "militia" historically refers to the people at large, armed and ready to defend their homeland and their freedom with weapons supplied by themselves. Title 10, Section 311 of the

U.S. Code states: "The Militia of the United States consists of all able-bodied males at least 17 years of age. . . ." Moreover, historical records, including Constitutional Convention debates and the Federalist Papers, clearly indicate that the purpose of the Second Amendment was not to create a standing army, but to guard against the tyranny that the framers of the Constitution feared could be perpetrated by any professional armed body of government. It should be noted here that the arms, records, and ultimate control of the National Guard today lie with the Federal Government. This is the very condition the founding fathers warned against.

In Federalist Paper No. 29, for example, Alexander Hamilton assured the people that the army would always be a "select corps of moderate size" and that the "people at large [were] properly armed" to serve as a fundamental check against the standing army, the most dreaded of institutions. James Madison, in Federalist Paper No. 46, further promised the American people that, unlike the governments of Europe which were "afraid to trust the people with arms," the American people would continue under the new Constitution to possess "the advantage of being armed," and thereby would continually be able to form the Militia when needed as a "barrier against the enterprises of despotic ambition."

The case of *United States* v. *Miller* is frequently cited as a definite ruling that the right to keep and bear arms is a collective right, protecting the organized state militia—now the National Guard—rather than the individual right to own guns. But that was not the issue in *United States* v. *Miller* and no such ruling was made.

While such a decision was sought by the Justice Department, which was the *only* party presenting an argument in the case, the Court decided only that the National Firearms Act of 1934 was constitutional *in the absence of evidence to the contrary*. The case hinged on the narrow question of whether a sawed-off shotgun was suitable for militia use, and its ownership by individuals thus protected by the Second Amendment. The Court ruled that: "In the absence of [the presentation of] any evidence tending to show that possession or use of a 'shotgun having a barrel of less than eighteen inches in length' at this time has some reasonable relationship to the preservation or efficiency of a well-regulated militia, we cannot say that the Second Amendment guarantees the right to keep and bear such an instrument. Certainly it is not within judicial notice that this weapon is any part of the military equipment or that its use could contribute to the common defense."

Because no evidence or argument was presented by other than the Justice Department, the Court was not made aware that some 30,000 short-barreled shotguns were used as "trench guns" during World War I, nor could it have known that similar guns would be used in World War II and Vietnam.

The Supreme Court has ruled on only three other cases raising the Second Amendment—all during the last half of the nineteenth century. In each of these cases, the Court held that the Second Amendment only applied to actions of the federal government, not of private individuals (*U.S.* v. *Cruikshank*, 1876) or state governments (*Presser* v. *Illinois*, 1886 and *Miller* v. *Texas*, 1894). At the same time, the Court also held, in *Presser*, that the First Amendment guarantee of freedom of assembly did not apply to the states; and in *Miller* v. *Texas*, it held that the Fourth amendment guarantee against unreasonable search and seizures did not apply to the states, since the Court believed that all the amendments comprising the Bill of Rights were limitations solely on the powers of Congress, not upon the powers of the states.

It was not until two generations later that the Court began to rule, under the Fourteenth Amendment, that the First, Fourth, and various other provisions of the Bill of Rights limited both Congress and state legislatures. No similar decision concerning the Second Amendment has ever been made in spite of contemporary scholarship proving conclusively that the purpose of the Fourteenth Amendment was to apply all of the rights in the Bill of Rights to the states. That research proves that the Fourteenth Amendment was made a part of the constitution to prevent states from depriving the newly-freed slaves of the rights guaranteed in the Bill of Rights, including what the Supreme Court's *Dred Scott* decision referred to as one of the rights of citizens, the right "to keep and carry arms wherever they went."

MYTH: "A person in a public place with a gun and without a permit is looking for trouble."

Gun prohibitionists have seized on this myth to back legislative/administrative proposals to penalize and discourage gun ownership by imposing a mandatory prison term on persons carrying or possessing firearms without proper authorization. Massachusetts' Bartley-Fox Law and New York's Koch-Carey law are premier examples of the current "gun control" strategy. Such legislation is detrimental only to peaceful citizens, not criminals.

By the terms of such a mandatory or increased sentence proposal, the unlicensed carrying of a firearm—no matter how innocent the circumstances—is penalized by a six to twelve month jail sentence. It would be imposed on citizens although in many areas it is virtually impossible for persons to obtain a carry permit. Thus it is not difficult to contemplate circumstances which would extenuate such a sentence: fear of crime, arbitrary denial of authorization and red-tape delay in obtaining official permission to carry a firearm, or misunderstanding of the numerous and vague laws governing the transportation of firearms.

The potential for unknowingly or unwittingly committing a technical violation of a licensing law is enormous. Myriad legal definitions of "carrying" vary from state to state, and city to city, including most transportation of firearms—accessible or not, loaded or not, in a trunk or case. And out-of-state travelers are exceedingly vulnerable because of these various definitions.

It is necessary only to look at the first persons arrested under the Massachusetts and New York "mandatory penalty" laws for proof that such laws are misdirected: an elderly woman passing out religious pamphlets in a dangerous section of Boston, and an Ohio truck driver coming to the aid of a woman apparently being kidnapped in New York City.

In New York City—prior to the enactment of the Koch-Carey mandatory sentence for possession law—the bureaucratic logjam in the licensing division, combined with a soaring crime rate, forced law-abiding citizens to obtain a gun illegally for self-protection. In effect, citizens admitted that they would rather risk a mandatory penalty for illegally owning a firearm than risk their lives and property at the hands of New York's violent, uncontrolled criminals. Literally, honest citizens feared the streets more than the courtrooms.

In contrast, the city's criminal element faces no similar threat of punishment. A report carried in the March 1, 1984, issue of The New York *Times* says it all: "Conviction on felony charges is rare. Because of plea-bargaining, the vast majority of those arrested on felony charges are tried on lesser, misdemeanor charges."

Of 106,171 felony arrests in 1983, only 25,987 were indicted on felony charges, with 20,641 resulting in convictions.

Yet, under a mandatory or increased penalty for carrying law, gun owners are treated separately and distinctly as being more dangerous and more of a threat to society than perpetrators of violent crimes—simply for possessing or carrying a firearm without the requisite papers. In championing New York's tough Koch-Carey law, Mayor Ed Koch said contemptuously of gun owners, "Nice guys who own guns aren't nice guys." No such rancor was expressed about the city's criminal justice system where the chances of hardened criminals being arrested on felony charges are one in one hundred. And the chance of any given felony arrest ending in a prison sentence is one out of 108, according to a January 4, 1981, New York *Times* article.

In essence, a mandatory or increased sentence for firearms carrying convolutes the criminal justice system by making gun owners "criminals" subject to a severe, fixed jail sentence while murderers, robbers, rapists, drug pushers and "white collar" or corporate thieves often go free.

Indeed, a 1982 National Institute of Justice study of Massachusetts' Bartley-Fox law concludes: " . . . the effect may be to penalize some less serious offenders, while the punishment for more serious cases is postponed, reduced or avoided altogether . . . it is difficult, perhaps fundamentally impossible, to substantiate the popular claim that mandatory sentencing is an effective tool for reducing crime."

Most prosecutors and judges in New York, according to a study funded by the U.S. Department of Justice, rarely use the Koch-Carey law. Nevertheless, more people without criminal records are being arrested and prosecuted than before the law took effect, diverting police from violent criminals to surveillance of citizens. Laws like Bartley-Fox and Koch-Carey are infrequently used against violent criminals who face longer sentences for robbery or assault. And, they are less likely to be punished than before the laws took effect.

Such legislation invites police routinely to stop and frisk people randomly on the street on suspicion of firearms possession. In fact, the Police Foundation has called for the random use of metal detectors on the streets to apprehend people carrying firearms without authorization. In waiving the constitutionally guaranteed right to privacy, police would be empowered under the Police

Foundation's blueprint for disarmament to "systematically stop a certain percentage of people on the streets . . . in business neighborhoods and run the detectors by them, just as you do at the airport. If the detectors produce some noise then that might establish probable cause for a search."

While admitting that such "police state" tactics would require "methods . . . that liberals instinctively dislike," government researchers James Q. Wilson and Mark H. Moore called for more aggressive police patrolling in public places, saying: "To inhibit the carrying of handguns, the police should become more aggressive in stopping suspicious people and, where they have reasonable grounds for their suspicions, frisking (i.e., patting down) those stopped to obtain guns. Hand-held magnet meters, of the sort used by airport security guards, might make the street frisks easier and less obtrusive. All this can be done without changing the law." (The Washington *Post*, April 1, 1981) Note, they said "people," not criminals.

In conclusion, mandatory or increased penalties for possession laws can only have the effect of creating scores of artificial gun-law criminals without disarming roughly 50,000 gun-wielding criminals who are terrorizing society. And its enforcement requires draconian punishment, a massive increase in the number of police, judges and prisons, violations of constitutional rights to privacy and against unreasonable searches and seizures, or more likely, a combination of all three.

Clearly, instead of imposing further penalties upon the law-abiding gun owner and gun purchaser, the proper approach is to impose mandatory punishment for the use of deadly weapons in the commission of violent crime.

The remedy, or any appropriate penalty, must be after the commission of an offense if the presumption of innocence is to be preserved.

MYTH: "Gun laws reduce crime."

The greatest myth perpetrated by the advocates of repressive gun laws is that such laws reduce crime. They do not.

No empirical study of the effectiveness of gun laws has shown any positive effect—although, to the dismay of the prohibitionists, such studies have shown a negative effect. That is, in areas having lower levels of private firearms ownership, the robbery rates are almost invariably higher, presumably because criminals are aware that their intended victims are less likely to have the means with which to defend themselves.

Further, of all the gun laws enacted in the past 10 to 20 years—each promised by its advocates to result in a reduction of crime—not one city, not one state, not one nation, has experienced a reduction in crime rates, nor even a reduced rate of crime growth in comparison to its neighboring cities and states and nations without such laws.

If gun laws worked, the proponents of such laws would gleefully cite examples of lessened crime. Instead, they uniformly blame the absence of tougher or wider spread measures for the failures of the laws they advocated. Or they cite denials of license applications as evidence the law is doing something beyond preventing honest citizens from being able legally to acquire a firearm. And they cite two jurisdictions' gun laws as "working"—Massachusetts and the District of Columbia. Yet crime in Washington rose dramatically between 1976, the year before its handgun ban took effect, and 1982, the year the city's voters adopted an NRA-endorsed mandatory penalty for misuse of guns in violent crimes. The violent crime rate rose 43% during those years, and the murder rate rose 14%, while the national rates were rising 20% and 3%, respectively. After adopting a law to punish violent criminals, Washington's crime trends have been similar to the nation's.

With a crime rate rising twice as fast as big cities overall, Washington could not even claim a relative change in gun use in criminal violence. No wonder D.C. Police Chief Maurice Turner said, "What had the gun control law done to keep criminals from getting guns? Absolutely nothing. . . . [City residents] ought to have the opportunity to have a handgun."

Massachusetts is an odd example for anti-gunners to choose, since the much vaunted Bartley-Fox law did not make it more difficult to obtain or carry any firearm legally; it made mandatory a one-year mandatory penalty for carrying a firearm without proper authority. For a time, gun related street robberies rose, and non-gun crimes skyrocketed. Generally, however, the murder-rate fluctuations in the Bay State have mirrored national trends with other violent crimes increasing somewhat faster than in the nation as a whole.

The major visible effect of gun laws is an obvious burden upon the law-abiding, who pay for the follies of their lawmakers by spending time, money and effort to overcome bureaucratic red tape in order to continue owning and enjoying their guns. Needless to say, the criminal does not bother with the niceties of obeying the law—for a criminal is by definition, someone who disobeys laws.

There is another visible effect of gun laws, one that burdens the tax-paying public. Gun laws must be administered by bureaucrats who provide nothing productive while draining the public treasury. Further, such laws are implemented and enforced by the law enforcement officers who could far better spend their time and talents in the pursuit of criminals rather than in investigations of the law-abiding and prosecutions for victimless crimes such as simple possession or carrying of a firearm.

Furthermore, restrictive gun laws create a Catch-22 for victims of violent crime. Under court decisions, the police have no legal obligation to protect any particular individual, and under restrictive gun laws, it may be illegal for the person to protect himself. A citizen is thus in the position of having to give up effective self-protection or risk arrest if he or she successfully wards off a violent criminal. In Washington, D.C., according to the author and key supporter of their gun law, self-defense use of handguns has fallen 62% since the virtual handgun ban was put into effect.

But there is an invisible effect of gun laws that may prove far more important than the visible, direct costs—that is, the social costs of increasing numbers of normally law-abiding citizens disobeying unpopular, irritating or expensive gun laws. Such high social cost was paid during the era of the prohibition of alcohol when a significant portion, if not the majority of drinkers, simply ignored Federal law. The era produced a generation of scofflaws, and provided fertile ground for the growth of organized crime syndicates that plague the nation a half-century later.

The evidence that gun laws are creating scofflaws is evident to anyone willing to look. In New York City, police estimate that there are two million illegal guns—and only 60,000 legally owned handguns. In Chicago, a recent mandatory registration law has resulted in compliance by only a fraction of those who had previously registered their guns. The same massive non-compliance—not by criminals, whom no one expects will comply, but by the particular minority groups fearful of repression—is evident wherever stringent gun laws are enacted.

In exchange for such high costs, what have the nation's lawmakers achieved? Not an instance of a reduction in crimes of violence. There is evidence of increases in robberies and other offenses where potential victims are disarmed by governmental fiat.

And laws addressed directly to the question of misuse do work. When stiff, certain punishment is levied upon those who misuse firearms—even when it is merely threatened—crime rates go down, particularly for predatory crimes like murder and robbery.

After adopting a mandatory penalty for using a firearm in the commission of a violent crime in 1975, Virginia's murder rate dropped 38% and robbery 24% in 11 years. South Carolina recorded a 41% murder rate decline between 1975 and 1986, and a 10% robbery rate drop, with a similar law. Other impressive declines in homicide rates were recorded in other states using mandatory penalties, such as Arkansas (down 28% in 11 years), Delaware (down 29% in 14 years), Montana (down 42% in 10 years), and Maryland (down 28% in 14 years). At almost the same time, Georgia adopted both a mandatory penalty for criminal misuse of firearms and a system making it easier for law-abiding citizens lawfully to carry handguns; between 1976 and 1986, Georgia recorded a 19% drop in its homicide rate, better than three times the regional decline and eight times the national.

Yet in none of these areas has the mandatory sentencing been fully implemented, due to the reluctance of prosecutors and judges to give up their discretionary authority. Thus far, such astounding reductions in crime are due mainly to the threat of punishment—once the criminals become convinced that they need to have no more fear of committing crimes with a gun than any other weapon, crime will again climb.

There is ample evidence that there is a solution to the crime problem, and a solution to the problem of criminal misuse of guns. That solution lies in the *promise*, not the mere threat, of swift, certain punishment. So long as the lawmakers refuse to apply that solution, and instead attempt to control crime by controlling law-abiding gun owners, the nation's problems with crime and criminals will only increase.

Our challenge: To reform and strengthen our federal and state criminal justice systems. We must bring about a sharp reversal in the trend toward undue leniency and "revolving door justice." We must insist upon speedier trials and upon punishments which are commensurate with the crimes. Rehabilitation should be tempered with a realization that not all can be rehabilitated.

The job ahead will not be an easy one. The longer gun control advocates distract the nation from this task by embracing that single siren song, the longer it will take and the more difficult our job will be. Beginning is the hardest step, and the NRA Institute has taken it. Join NRA. Support ILA. Work with us. We need your help.

A QUESTION OF SELF-DEFENSE[5]

"Tell them what rape is. Be graphic. Be disgusting. Be obscene. Make them sick. If they throw up, then they have the tiniest idea of what it is."

Those were the words of a young Boston woman to a reporter researching an article on Bostonians arming themselves for self-defense. The woman had been raped. The police responded quickly. They responded after the woman telephoned. After the rape. After the assailant left.

Three women from Washington, D.C. fared worse than the woman from Boston.

The women shared a three-story house in a crime-plagued section of the Northwest quadrant of the city. Early one March morning in 1975 two men broke into the home. They discovered one woman and her four-year-old daughter asleep in their second floor bedroom. The woman was forced to sodomize one man. She was raped by the other.

Her screams awoke the two women in the third floor bedroom. They telephoned the police. Within three minutes, four Metropolitan police cruisers were dispatched to the scene. The two women crawled out of their room onto an adjoining roof.

[5]Reprint of a pamphlet by the National Rifle Association. Reprinted by permission.

They watched as the police approached the house. One officer knocked on the front door. No answer. Five minutes later, the officers left.

Inside the house, the woman on the second floor again screamed. Again, the women on the floor above crawled into the house and called the police. Again, they were assured that help was on the way.

That help never arrived. The dispatcher never alerted patrolling officers.

Soon the intruders discovered the other women. At knife point for the next 14 hours, the three women were raped, robbed, beaten and forced to commit sexual acts upon each other and with their assailants.

The Court's Response

The three, spared their lives at least, sued the District of Columbia police. They lost.

The District of Columbia Court of Appeals offered *"our sympathy for appellants who were the tragic victims of despicable criminal acts."*

Nevertheless the panel of judges found that " . . . the District of Columbia appears to follow the well-established rule that official police personnel and the government employing them are not generally liable to victims of criminal acts for failure to provide adequate police protection . . . **this uniformly accepted rule rests upon the fundamental principle that a government and its agents are under no general duty to provide public services, such as police protection, to any particular individual citizen** . . . a publicly maintained police force constitutes a basic governmental service provided to benefit the community at large by promoting public peace, safety and good order."

No word from the court addressed the internal peace or safety of the women forced to live with the nightmare of their 14-hour ordeal. Nothing addressed the effect on the four-year-old child.

What happened in the District of Columbia's Court to the three brutalized women and the child was not an isolated incident.

On February 18, 1982, the Court of Appeals for the State of New York handed down a decision that chilled New York's subway passengers.

Two suits against the New York City Transit Authority charged the agency with negligence for not taking steps to correct conditions it, the Authority, knew presented a clear danger to passengers. In one incident, a woman was raped in a subway station that was the scene of four separate rapes over a span of a few months. The second involved a retired school board official who was robbed and injured by knife-wielding thugs at a stop where 13 separate robberies (eight with knives) occurred over a ten-month period.

The court dismissed both.

The court ruled that the Transit Authority was free from liability just as was any municipality or governmental agency. The Transit Authority had no responsibility *"to protect a person on its premises from assault by a third person"* nor did it have an obligation to increase police protection for well-documented high crime areas within the subway system, according to the court.

The cold, harsh legal facts are that by statute and court decree, local and state governments and "their agents," the police, have no obligation to provide protection for the individual.

Legal technicalities notwithstanding, the police do attempt to protect the public to the extent that the law and their resources allow.

In the opinion of nationally syndicated columnist Joseph Kraft, "the explosion in crime has literally overwhelmed the police. Without a major increase in numbers they are condemned to a losing battle." Given the reality of their numbers, the protection afforded by law enforcement is often woefully inadequate, a point well noted by Florida officials.

Jim Smith, then Attorney General of Florida, told state legislators that of some 700,000 calls for help by citizens to Dade County authorities in 1981, only 200,000 received any police response. *A half million Dade County residents' pleas for police aid went unanswered.*

Smith paused, then answered the question raised by the press and politicos regarding "why everybody in Dade County goes out and buys a gun."

"They damn well better. They've got to protect themselves," said Attorney General Smith.

His words were echoed later that year by the head of the Dade County Police Benevolent Association.

Civilians Armed for Self-Defense

The very concept strikes at the heart of the debate, pro and con, over the private ownership of firearms.

Today, in particular, the focus of the controversy has been primarily on handguns. Each argument, each consideration seems to raise yet another question.

Government research indicates that the majority of firearms owned by Americans are owned for sport and recreational purposes rather than for self-protection, by a rate of three-to-one. The increase in gun sales seem to be people who already own one or more guns rather than among non–gun owning families. *However, among the 10 to 15 million women handgun owners, the figures favor self-protection as the main reason for owning a gun in urban areas.*

What thoughts run through a woman's mind, particularly after an assault or attempted assault, when she considers owning or using a gun for protection?

Do they differ from those of a male?

Does a handgun provide real or imagined security for the woman living alone . . . for the merchant in a high crime area . . . for families with small children?

Are handguns more of a danger to their owners than to criminals?

Are they "accidents waiting to happen"?

On the negative side is the notion that handguns should be banned to the average citizen. Proponents of this position will concede restricted use of handguns by on-duty military, police and private security personnel. Civilian competitive pistol shooters could continue their sport on the condition that their handguns would be stored in "armories" and not at home. Hunting with handguns, legal in 49 states, is simply ignored by opponents to private handgun ownership. Handguns for protection would not be allowed.

Ironically, police and military views of handguns are 180 degrees opposite to the rhetoric of such prohibitionists. The official view by police and the military is that their on- and off-duty handguns are strictly "defensive" arms. Rifles and shotguns are considered "offensive" implements.

Unresolved, too, is an apparent contradiction in the prohibitionists' line of argument. On one hand, they argue that the handgun, particularly when used by the criminal or the enraged family member, is the most lethal of instruments. On the other, they discount its protective value to the honest citizen because of what they describe as a handgun's "inherent inaccuracy."

Literally tens of millions of Americans disagree with the prohibitionist position. **They see their handguns as critical tools that might spell the difference between becoming the victim of a crime or the victor in a confrontation with a criminal predator.** Just what does the record show?

A Look at the Past

Protection of self, of one's loved ones, of one's home and community is the root of the American tradition of gun ownership. It is a concept cherished from the beginning of time and preserved most democratically within the English common law heritage where the defense of home, community and kingdom rested upon an armed and ready populace. This was a distinct divergence from the Continental practice of a disarmed peasantry "protected" by the armed knights of the nobility.

Sir William Blackstone's "Commentaries," upon which the American legal system is based, described "the right of having and using arms for self-preservation and defense" as among the "Absolute Rights of Individuals."

Self-defense, said Sir William, was "justly called the primary law of nature, so it is not, neither can it be in fact, taken away by the laws of society."

What the Law Says

Gun ownership by convicted felons, drug addicts and court-ruled mental defectives is currently forbidden by federal law. That law and more than 20,000 state and local laws not only forbid criminal purchase of, possession of and use of all rifles, handguns and shotguns by these people, but they also levy prison and/or monetary penalties against anyone misusing firearms in any manner. These laws are in addition to laws against murder, robbery, rape, etc.

Nevertheless, the push for yet more layers of federal, state and local law continues. With virtually every imaginable criminal act covered by existing law, the new suggestions invariably focus on restricting the non-criminal acquisition, possession and use of firearms, handguns in particular. Toward this end, the idea of handgun use for self-protection is continually dismissed.

Victims Turned Victors

Shortly after her husband left for work, a Waco, Texas, housewife heard the front door window break. A strange man reached in, unlocked the door, and entered the front room.

The housewife ran to the bedroom. She locked the door and grabbed a handgun kept beneath the mattress. The intruder kicked in the door. He saw the gun aimed at him. He left.

Twice a 51-year-old Los Angeles, California woman had been raped by the same man. He had not yet been apprehended. After the second assault, she purchased a handgun. The man returned a third time. His criminal career came to an abrupt end.

Masquerading as a police officer, a man raped a Baltimore, Maryland, woman in front of her two children, ages one and two. When he threatened the oldest child, the woman lunged for a hidden revolver. It was the last thing the rapist saw.

When Phoenix, Arizona, authorities responded to a breaking-and-entering call, they found a 77-year-old woman gently rocking in her favorite chair. Her favorite .38 revolver was pointed at a man obediently lying half in and half out of her "pet door."

Those four incidents are not uncommon.

Four public opinion surveys (commissioned separately by the California Justice Department, two handgun prohibitionist groups and the National Rifle Association) verified that 600 to 1,000 Americans use handguns in defensive situations a day. *Three percent of the U.S. adult population or 4.8 million people acknowledged that they had used a handgun for defense. Nine percent or 8.5 million people stated that they had been in situations where they felt they needed a handgun but had none available.*

Since the night two decades ago when more than a score of neighbors watched as New York crime victim Kitty Genovese was slashed to death, headlines across the nation appear to be charting a new trend. Apathy and the attitude that the safety of neighbors and one's neighborhood is the job of the police and not of the community **together with the police** seems to be giving ground to a resurgence of community involvement.

In fact, criminologists and police nationwide credit crime drops in the 1980s to increased community involvement.

In Baltimore, a 1979 *Evening Sun* headline ran: "Lady D.A. Outshoots Thugs." Chicago's *Tribune* chronicled one "Gunman Becomes the Victim" to an armed homeowner in 1982. Georgia's Atlanta *Constitution/Journal* ran the headline "Burglaries Fall in DeKalb (County) as Victims Take Aim" in 1982.

Esquire magazine ran two articles in defense of handgun ownership in 1981. And, the trend toward citizens armed for defense was cover story material in *Woman's Day* (1983), *Boston Magazine* (1982), Philadelphia's *Today Magazine* (1982) and in *Savvy Magazine* (1981).

Television's popular talkshow host Phil Donahue was surprised at the audience's reaction to his attempt to discount handguns as useful self-defense aids. He was hooted by his largely female audience with taunts that he had "never been raped."

Had Donahue read *Glamour* magazine's readership survey in May of 1981 he would have known that 65 percent of *Glamour* readers said they own guns; 66 percent of those owned primarily for self-defense. Sixty-eight percent opposed banning handguns.

Who Gets Hurt?

The idea that a potential crime victim runs a greater risk of injury if he or she is armed has been proven groundless.

According to U.S. Justice Department victimization studies, a citizen who uses arms stands not only a greater chance of avoiding injury than his or her unarmed counterpart, but also increases his or her odds of foiling the criminal assault.

The Justice Department data show that during a robbery attempt, one of every three *unarmed* victims is injured. On the other hand, only one in seven *armed* victims is injured. This means that an honest citizen who is armed reduces his or her chances of being injured by one half.

More incidents of victims' successful use of guns would occur, and would be reported to the police, if there were fewer laws against carrying firearms.

A 26-city survey by the Justice Department found that of 32,000 attempted rapes, 32 percent were actually committed. Only three percent of attempted rapes succeeded when the woman defended herself with a knife or gun.

Criminal Risk?

Criminals face greater risk of injury from armed citizens than police, according to available Justice Department data.

One glaring statistic is that burglars who choose, either unintentionally or otherwise, to ply their trade in occupied homes are twice as likely to be shot or killed as they are to be caught, convicted and imprisoned by the U.S. criminal justice system.

Armed citizens kill two to three times the number of criminals killed each year by law enforcement. No studies have been conducted on the numbers of criminals wounded, frightened off or held for authorities by armed citizens.

None of this has been lost on the typical criminal.

Research gathered by Professors James Wright and Peter Rossi, co-authors of the U.S. Justice Department's benchmark three-year study of weapons and criminal violence in America, points to the armed citizen or the threat of the armed citizen as possibly the most effective crime deterrent in the nation.

Wright and Rossi questioned over 1,800 prisoners serving time in prisons across the nation. They found:

• *85 percent agreed that the "smart criminal" will attempt to find out if a potential victim is armed.*

• *75 percent felt that burglars avoided occupied dwellings for fear of being shot.*

• *60 percent felt that the typical criminal feared being shot by citizens more than he feared being shot by police.*

• *80 percent of "handgun predators" had encountered armed citizens.*

• *53 percent did not commit a specific crime for fear that the victim was armed.*

• *57 percent of "handgun predators" were scared off or shot at by armed victims.*

Where Criminals Fear to Tread

The classic example of the threat of armed citizens to criminals and the corresponding effect on an area's crime rate remains Orlando, Florida.

In 1966, rape in that city skyrocketed from 12.8 per 100,000 citizens in 1965 to 35.9 per 100,000. The Orlando police organized a handgun training program for women. The program ran from October 1966 through April 1967. The media gave extraordinary coverage to the fact that Orlando's female population was armed and more than willing to resist criminal attack.

One year later, Orlando's rape rate plummetted to 4.1 per 100,000. Elsewhere in the state (excluding Orlando) rape rates increased that year.

Other areas which saw similar crime drops for armed robbery or rape after instituting well-publicized firearm training programs for merchants or women were Detroit and Highland Park, Michigan, and Montgomery, Alabama.

What about Accidents or Arguments in the Home?

Fear that handguns are somehow home accident or "crime of passion" catalysts are unfounded in view of research into both areas.

Criminologist James Wright described the typical incident of family violence as "that mythical crime of passion" on a television documentary, "Gunfight, USA" aired over the Public Broadcasting System in 1983.

Wright denied that the typical "crime of passion" was an isolated incident by otherwise normally placid and loving individuals. The available research showed that it was in fact "the culminating event in a long history of interpersonal violence between the parties."

Wright further noted that handguns did not play the aggressive role most often attributed to them.

"The common pattern, the more common pattern, is for wives to shoot their husbands. Proportionately, men kill their women by other means, more brutal means, more degrading means. To deny that woman the right to own the firearm is in some sense to guarantee in perpetuity to her husband the right to beat her at will," said Wright.

It should be repeated that these men who kill their spouses are not "nice" folks.

Many of the homicides listed by the FBI as occurring between relatives, neighbors and acquaintances are not simple domestic squabbles.

Homicide by street gang members of rival gang members, homicide between drug traffickers, organized crime "hits," slayings of neighbors by the neighborhood criminal predator are all listed as "non-felony homicides." They are included in the "relative, friend, acquaintance, neighbor" categories that are used by handgun prohibitionists to inflate "crime of passion" statistics.

As "accidents waiting to happen" handguns once again appear to bear the brunt of unfair and unwarranted rhetoric.

The National Safety Council *does not* break down incidents of handgun versus rifle or shotgun related accidental deaths. Research now underway at Florida State University suggests long guns are involved in a majority of the 1,800 accidental firearm-related deaths logged in the U.S. annually. That research also indicates that a sizable number of those deaths are, in fact, not accidents but well-disguised homicides or suicides. Alcohol also seems to play a disproportionately large factor in the overall accidental death toll (50 percent).

Since Prohibition, the rate of firearm-related accidental deaths in the U.S. has been on the decline.

At its highest (during Prohibition) the rate was 2.5 per 100,000 citizens. It leveled out at 0.8 per 100,000 since 1978 before falling to 0.7 in 1985.

A Record for Safety

The American public should be commended for its long record of safe firearms handling. Credit, too, should be given to training programs such as those offered by the National Rifle Association, an organization which has pioneered the field of safe firearms handling and training for more than a century.

The first hunter safety program was introduced by the NRA in 1949. Over the next few years, the accidental firearms death rate dropped to 1.6 per 100,000. Hunter safety is now taught by the fish and wildlife departments of all 50 states. The result of such training is evident.

The most recent program introduced by the NRA is the Voluntary Practical Firearms Program. This program, taught by NRA certified instructors nationwide, is aimed at individuals, women in particular, who feel they want a handgun for self-protection.

NRA instructors teach the principles of safe firearms handling and marksmanship excellence to hundreds of thousands of civilians and police each year.

A Matter of Choice

It is not the intention of the NRA to suggest that handguns are the only means of self-defense. Nor is it the NRA's intention to suggest that handguns should be purchased for this purpose.

The question of handgun ownership is one that is highly personal. It is a choice that should be made by the individual. It is a choice that should not be forbidden to the honest citizen by an overprotective government, particularly one which has no responsibility to provide real protection when one's life is threatened. It is a choice that should be approached with information and not emotion.

The purpose of the self-defense handgun is to preserve life and to discourage criminal violence. It may well prove to be the most immediate means of thwarting criminal activity. In that sense, it serves to provide security in a manner similar to health or life insurance. If ever there arises that time when it is needed, no substitute will do.

GAGA OVER GUNS[6]

Pardon us for writing about gun control again, but we didn't bring it up. President Reagan did, and even though he ought to know better, he's still against it. This was the burden of his recent speech to the convention of the National Rifle Association in Phoenix, a speech that pandered to its audience without a trace

[6]Editorial. Reprinted by permission from *New Republic*, My. 30, '83, pp. 9–10. Copyright © 1983 by *New Republic*.

of shame. A sample of the President's chilling treasurer's-report prose: "I'm also happy to report that since I took office the sale of M-1 rifles to participants and instructors in high-power rifle marksmanship training programs has been increased significantly. I have asked the Department of Defense to look at ways in which sales might be increased further." (How about getting the boys at D.O.D. to open a retail outlet at the Texas School Book Depository?)

To those who worry about being killed by gun-wielding criminals, Mr. Reagan offers a peculiar sort of reassurance. "We will never disarm any American who seeks to protect his or her family from fear and harm," he said stoutly. It takes no great philosophical insight to understand that this statement proceeds from premises that are profoundly wrong. In a civilized society, physical security is a collective responsibility, not an individual one. Armed families cannot substitute for the police power of a democratic state, and they should not be necessary as a supplement to it. What the President is proposing here is a policy of detterence at the family level. Your only protection against somebody else's gun is a gun of your own; if you don't have a gun you are not just a normal citizen but rather someone who has been "disarmed." Implicit in all this is a certain vision of American society. It's a Hollywood vision—but it doesn't come from the innocent Hollywood of Mickey Rooney, Frank Capra, or, for that matter, Ronald Reagan. It's the despairing vigilante vision of *Straw Dogs* and *Death Wish* and *The Road Warrior*—and of *Taxi Driver*, the movie that inspired John W. Hinckley Jr.—and it's not what the social contract is about.

Mr. Reagan quoted the Second Amendment to the Constitution the way the N.R.A. likes to hear it quoted. "The Constitution says,' . . . the right of the people to keep and bear arms, shall not be infringed,'" he said. The ploy represented by those three dots is beginning to wear thin. The full text of the Amendment—"A well regulated militia, being necessary to the security of a free State, the right of the people to keep and bear arms, shall not be infringed"—is not so awfully long. But Mr. Reagan didn't leave out the first half to save time. He left it out to save face, his and the N.R.A.'s. Something like thirty thousand Americans die of gunshot wounds each year. Whatever else the people pulling the triggers may be, they do not constitute a well-regulated militia.

The Second Amendment reflects the founders' fears of a standing army and their preference for a part-time citizen force. They were not trying to guarantee unregulated access to arms, as the N.R.A. seems to believe. When the Amendment was written, guns were the most fearsome weapons in existence. If the N.R.A. and the President really believed in the logic of their position, they would be proclaiming the right of individuals to buy artillery pieces and mortars. The fact that they aren't is evidence that constitutional cant aside, the debate is really about where you draw the line.

The way Mr. Reagan draws it, machine guns are probably out, but some surprising things are in—armor-piercing bullets, for example. In his N.R.A. speech he boasted of "our efforts for a minimum mandatory term of five years' imprisonment for the use of armor-piercing bullets, cop-killer bullets, during a federal crime of violence," a dodge that should fool no one. These bullets have no sporting or other legitimate purpose; their only use is to kill people who are wearing bulletproof vests, and they should be banned. They would be banned under a bill sponsored by Senator Daniel Patrick Moynihan and by Representative Mario Biaggi, who used to be a cop. It's a very modest bill—it shows how little the advocates of gun control are really asking—but the gun nuts are against it, and so is the President. So much for the war on crime.

The Biaggi-Moynihan bill ought to be what politicians call a motherhood issue. How can anyone possibly be *for* the sale of "cop-killer bullets"? Yet the bill has only eight cosponsors in the Senate and ninety-seven in the House. This is a measure of the fear generated by the N.R.A. and the rest of the gun lobby, despite the large popular majority in favor of much more severe forms of gun control that invariably shows up in public opinion clothes. With a change of heart—and God knows he had the occasion for one—Ronald Reagan would have been the perfect President to galvanize that majority. It didn't happen. The gun craziness can't go on forever; eventually, a President will come along who is willing and able to stop it. Meanwhile, bang bang.

SHOULD CONGRESS ADOPT
PROPOSED RELAXATION OF HANDGUN CONTROLS?[7]

PRO
by Hon. TED STEVENS
United States Senator, Alaska, Republican

*From the Senate floor debate of July 9, 1985, during consideration of
S. 49, the proposed Federal Firearms Owners' Protection Act.*

The Firearms Owners' Protection Act is at long last coming
before the full Senate for consideration. This is the most important piece of legislation for gun owners in this century. Since the
passage of the Gun Control Act of 1968, the erosion of the right
to keep and bear arms has been justified on the basis that rigid
gun control laws will reduce the incidence of violent crime. However, the law has been ineffective. It has served to punish the law-
abiding gun owner for the actions of career criminals, and has
been implemented in a way that discourages gun ownership.

S. 49 focuses on areas of regulatory abuse resulting from the
Gun Control Act. An entire Federal agency spends a large portion of its effort in prosecuting and harassing gun owners for
technical violations of the law. Our tax dollars will be applied
more effectively if our law enforcement officials become more involved in detecting and arresting robbers, muggers, rapists, and
murderers.

There are a number of amendments which will be offered to
S. 49, most of which cloud the issue. For example, the imposition
of waiting periods on the sale of firearms does not add any deterrent quality. Career criminals will continue to skirt an established
screening process. The paperwork requirements and effort associated with waiting periods will divert personnel away from true
crime control efforts.

[7]Reprint of an article by U.S. Senators and Congressmen: Ted Stevens, Edward
Kennedy, Robert Dole, James A. McClure, Charles Mathias, Spark Matsunaga, Orrin Hatch, Carl Levin, Christopher Dodd, Robert Kasten, John Kerry, and Steven
Symms. Reprinted by permission from *Congressional Digest*, Vol. 65 (My. '86), pp.
138–59. Copyright © 1986 by *Congressional Digest*.

Even more troubling are the efforts to make a distinction between handguns and long guns such as rifles and shotguns. If we exempt handguns from the changes being sought by S. 49, we would accept the premise that possession alone is a serious cause of violent crime. Criminals are responsible for the violence in this country. Making a distinction between handguns and other firearms serves to restrict the constitutional right of citizens to keep and bear arms without deterring criminal behavior. It sets a dangerous precedent for future exclusion of other firearms classes.

Pervasive regulation is not the answer to the growing incidence of violent crime. The Gun Control Act has been in existence for almost 20 years, but crime has risen steadily. Our law enforcement efforts must be directed at deterring criminal behavior. Strong penalties are required to deter the use of firearms in Federal crimes. There must be an immediate response to acts of violent crime and treason. I have sponsored legislation which calls for death by firing squad when treasonous acts are perpetrated for monetary gain. Senator McClure should be commended for taking a tough stance on the use of firearms to commit crimes. The day career criminals begin to feel the full force of the law for their acts is the day that we can walk the streets in safety.

CON
by Hon. EDWARD M. KENNEDY
United States Senator, Massachusetts, Democrat

From the debate of July 9, 1985, on the floor of the U.S. Senate during consideration of S. 49, the pending Federal Firearms Owners' Protection Act. Sen. Kennedy was the author of a proposed amendment to continue the existing prohibition on interstate sales of handguns.

This Amendment, which I and my colleagues offer, does not change or improve upon existing laws—as much as I would like to do that—rather, it merely continues the existing law on the interstate sale of handguns, while relaxing those same laws on the sale of sporting weapons, rifles, and long guns.

As I indicated at the outset of this debate, I have been willing for many years to join the sponsors of this legislation in reducing unnecessary restrictions and regulations on the purchase and sale of rifles and shotguns for hunting and sporting purposes. But I believe we must, at a minimum, continue current law with respect to handgun sales.

Handgun control is an essential part of effective law enforcement. The ready availability of lethal, concealable handguns undermines the fundamental effort to protect citizens from violent crime. As the police have said in their statements instead of weakening handgun controls, we should be working to keep handguns from falling into the wrong hands without jeopardizing in any way the legitimate sporting interests of our citizens or their interest in self-defense.

We all share the basic goal of the sponsors of this bill—to remove unnecessary regulatory burdens on the purchase of firearms by hunters and others for sporting purposes, and by law-abiding citizens seeking weapons for self protection.

But we must not misuse this worthwhile goal as an excuse to weaken the law as it applies to the narrow category of handguns—especially snubbies and "Saturday night specials"—which have no legitimate sporting purpose and which are often used in crime.

Over the past 4 years I repeatedly tried to draw this distinction during the Judiciary Committee's consideration of this bill; Congress can—and should—deal differently with long guns than it does with handguns.

Yet, the pending bill goes far beyond this legitimate goal. Instead, it weakens both Federal as well as State laws governing the control of handguns.

This issue is not a concern of mine alone. It is a concern shared by all the major police and law enforcement associations in the United States.

The law enforcement community in this country—the police officers, the State troopers, the chiefs of police, and many other law enforcement officers—have all spoken in support of this amendment to maintain existing law on the interstate sale of handguns.

From their point of view, the issue is pure and simple, it is a law enforcement issue—a crime control issue.

For those who are literally on the firing line, this is not an issue of restricting hunters or legitimate handgun owners in our society. Rather, it is an issue of keeping handguns out of the wrong hands.

Let me say once again that I have no objection to relaxing current limitations on interstate sales of rifles and long guns, but what possible justification is there to relaxing existing controls—which are modest already—on the sale of handguns?

We know 50 percent of all homicides in the United States involve handguns compared to only 5 percent for rifles. We know that handguns, and particularly the "snubbies"—handguns with a barrel length of 3 inches or less—are the preferred instruments of criminals.

Why would we want to ease existing laws on their interstate sale and transfer? How does making "snubbies" easier to get advance the interests of hunters and sportsmen in our society?

The answer is that it makes no sense whatsoever—and that is the message that the police chiefs and troopers have tried to give us.

I urge my colleagues to heed their call—to view this amendment for what it is: An effort to maintain existing law enforcement tools on the sale of handguns in our society.

This is a fundamental law enforcement issue—as every Attorney General's Task Force on Crime has stated, including President Reagan's task force in 1981. If we fail to adopt this amendment, we will not only turn our backs against this long record, but against the advice—indeed, the pleas—of local law enforcement officers from across our country.

I urge the Senate to adopt this amendment that merely continues existing law—nothing more, nothing less.

Only about 5 percent of the homicides in the United States are from long guns, rifles, or shotguns. So we are prepared to see that we remove some of the kinds of restrictions that exist in current law that hinder or cause some inconvenience to hunters if we are able to keep existing law on handguns, snubbies, and Saturday night specials.

One of the reasons that this legislation is on the floor is because those who support it want to reduce red tape for all those local gun dealers all across this country. The supporters of this bill want to reduce the burden on those small shopkeepers from the Federal hand and from Federal intervention or inspection. But without this amendment, what does this legislation provide with regard to handguns?

Without this amendment, this legislation says in deleting clause A, paragraph 3, and inserting in lieu thereof the following: (a) Shall not apply to the sale of, delivery of any firearm to a resident of a State other than a State in which the licensee's place of business is located if the sale and delivery and receipt fully comply with the legal conditions of sale in both such States; that is, where it is legitimate in the State where the sale will take place and legitimate in the State where the individual is from.

Let's say that the dealer makes a mistake. Say he does not know, for example, if he sells to somebody in Maryland that there is a 7-day waiting period, or in Nevada at the current time if that person lives in Las Vegas, it is 72 hours, or if the person is from Wyoming it is a 48-hour time limitation, et cetera.

Then what happens to that dealer? It says over here on page 21 that anyone who violates the provisions of this chapter shall be fined not more than $5,000, or imprisoned not more than 5 years. That person commits a felony.

If you do not accept this amendment, you are saying to every dealer out in the West and the South that if they do not know everything that happens to be in these two books at least as of the time that they were produced—let the record show that there is more than 2,000 pages here—if they do not know it, they can be penalized for $5,000 and commit a felony.

I hope we accept this amendment, which responds to the legitimate law enforcement issues that have been raised by those that know more about it than any single Member of this body and who are, day in and day out, faced with the force of violence in our society—and we hear a great deal about that issue internationally and locally, they know what it means, and they have seen their colleagues that have been brutalized and murdered.

I just hope that in our concern both for law enforcement, in our concern about the regulatory burden that we are placing on individual dealers, and in our concern about the role of the Federal Government reaching out and providing inspections into all of these little, small towns, communities, and dealers all over this country—and the dangers which they are going to have, the burden that is going to be placed upon all of them—that the Senate go on record and support this amendment.

Finally, I want to stress that this amendment applies only to handguns—the snubbies, the Saturday night specials. There are no hunting purposes whatsoever—no hunting purpose whatsoever—for a Saturday night special. I have listened to those Members of the Senate try to make that case in the quiet of a committee meeting, and I have heard the snickers of those who would support such a Senator's amendment because there is no legitimate sporting purpose for a snubbie. You cannot hit anything accurately beyond a few feet. Then we hear about how

Bambi is hurt in the woods and they have to go up and use a Saturday night special in order to save Bambi from misery. I hope we are not going to hear that laughable argument on the floor of the U.S. Senate this afternoon.

The final point that I will make is that we will hear very shortly how we cannot really keep pistols and Saturday night specials out of the hands of the criminals. So why should we inconvenience the legitimate sportsman? You can use that argument. But I hope they will address that and maybe suggest some changes in the law's controls on prohibitive drugs. You cannot stop illegal drugs in our society. Then why not make those illegal drugs available to others as well? The American people have too much common sense to swallow such arguments. We do not possibly suggest because we pass a law against murder that we stop all murders. Of course we do not.

But what we hope to do is be able to reduce to some extent, and the chief enforcement officials understand this issue best, and understand it so well that they believe we can have some impact to some extent in reducing the handgun terror that exists in so many parts of this country and on the city streets of this Nation. That is really what we are debating here this afternoon. I hope this amendment will be accepted.

PRO
by Hon. ROBERT J. DOLE
United States Senator, Kansas, Republican

From the debate of June 24, 1985, on the floor of the U.S. Senate during consideration of S. 49, the proposed Federal Firearms Owners' Protection Act. Sen. Dole serves as Majority Leader of the Senate.

Experience over the years has amply demonstrated that the subject of gun control is one of the most emotionally charged and politically explosive issues of our time. This is especially true for Senators who are standing for reelection. Indeed, I would suggest that the Senators who take leading roles in this debate could be eligible for some new profile in courage awards.

In past Congresses, the Senator from Kansas was actively involved in consideration of gun control legislation by the Committee on the Judiciary. This Senator offered three gun control amendments on other pending Senate legislation which were favorably received by the Senate and have become law. One of these amendments related to .22 caliber rimfire ammunition. As a result, tens of thousands of gun dealers have been relieved from the onerous and totally unnecessary requirement of recording the sale of each and every box of .22 caliber ammunition that was sold.

A second amendment that allowed limited imports of foreign made firearms which was previously prohibited from importation, passed the Senate and became law last year. This amendment authorized the Secretary of the Treasury to allow importation of firearms having value to collectors no matter what their original place of manufacture might have been. This amendment became law last year as part of the trade amendments, and the Treasury Department has now issued implementing regulations. A third amendment, imposing minimum mandatory sentences on Federal felons who use body armor piercing ammunition in the commission of their crimes was enacted as part of the 1984 crime control package.

In addition, I recently corresponded with the Secretary of the Treasury concerning proposed Internal Revenue Service regulations on broker reporting rules being used as a vehicle for Federal registration of firearms. I was assured by Treasury that no such result was intended and the IRS agreed that its regulations would be inappropriate for this purpose.

While these amendments have helped to restore the balance between the constitutional right to keep and bear arms and legitimate law enforcement requirements, more remains to be done. Since 1979, the distinguished Senator from Idaho on behalf of himself and a majority of the Senate, including the Senator, have introduced and reintroduced legislation intended to correct major deficiencies and imbalances of the Gun Control Act of 1968.

S. 49, a bill to protect firearm owners' constitutional rights, civil liberties, and rights to privacy, represents fulfillment of a promise long due. When Congress enacted the Gun Control Act of 1968, it made a pledge in the preamble that the act was not meant to impose unnecessary burdens on law-abiding citizens with respect to lawful use of firearms. Over the passage of time, it became apparent that this pledge was not being observed. Several hearings before our Judiciary and Appropriations Committees have demonstrated that vague or overly broad provisions of the act have been used to harass or ruin law-abiding citizens. In

1968 the United States committed itself to avoiding such abuses. I repeat, the time has come to fulfill that commitment.

The abuses which have occurred are fully documented in the hearings which are set out in the committee report on this bill.

There is no reason to permit cases like these to occur. It is time for us to fulfill the pledge this Congress made in 1968, to ensure that our enactments are used only against bona fide criminals. The bill before us would go a long way toward achieving that end. It will not restrict legitimate law enforcement. It will restrict abuses of authority.

Protection of individual rights and establishment of realistic rules is precisely what S. 49 is about. It is equally important to know what it is not. S. 49 is not a firearms bill. It does not change the core of the Gun Control Act. Felons are still barred for the most part from gun ownership. In fact, S. 49 makes this even clearer. Recording and other requirements remain. S. 49 leaves the substance, but shifts procedures to assure that the substance is fairly applied. There may be those who dislike our citizens who choose to own firearms, whether for sporting use or self defense. But I trust even they would not endorse conviction of the innocent, or confiscation of property of a person who has been acquitted, or administrative trials where prosecutors sit as judges. I trust they would not maintain that a man who has been pardoned is still a felon, or that one who makes an inadvertent error should be branded with that status. This is not, properly speaking, a firearms bill. It is, as its title states, a bill to protect individual rights.

S. 49 is cosponsored by 48 Members of this body. It is substantially the same bill introduced by Senator McClure in the last Congress and approved by the Senate as an amendment to other legislation. These proposals have the endorsement of the Fraternal Order of Police and the National Sheriff's Association. The FOP, in particular, testified that it considered this legislation: "A vast improvement over the Gun Control Act as it now exists. It clarifies, tightens and makes rational the all too often vague and inconsistent provisions of the act. We therefore support it from our standpoint as law enforcement professionals."

To be sure, S. 49 is not a special favor to the Fraternal Order of Police. Neither is it a special favor to firearms owners. It is simply a matter of common sense and individual rights—two matters which we owe to all citizens.

During the last Congress, this bill secured that endorsement of the Fraternal Order of Police and the National Sheriff's Association, two of our largest law enforcement groups. The National Sheriff's Association, which has a membership of over 65,000 sheriffs and deputies, testified that the bill is the needed change at the needed time. The Fraternal Order of Police, on behalf of over 60,000 policemen, testified that it strongly endorses the bill because its effect is to reform the Gun Control Act in ways that make it more rational, more clear, more narrowed and more precise—in a phrase, more enforceable. If we vote in accord with the endorsements of the Fraternal Order of Police and the National Sheriff's Association, it is hardly likely we vote for a measure that will harm law enforcement.

Of course, it should be noted that there are national police organizations who do not share this view. To them and other concerned individuals and organizations I suggest that the measure before us has received close scrutiny by the Departments of Justice and Treasury. Numerous changes have been made to accommodate legitimate law enforcement concerns. These changes were worked out in the course of extensive discussions and negotiations. It is my view that now is the time for the Senate to work its will on this controversial issue. Every attempt has been made to accommodate opposing views. While this year's version of McClure-Volkmer has been held at the desk, there is a long record of correction and refinement of this legislation.

In conclusion I urge speedy adoption of S. 49 by the Senate. I feel sure that when the Senate concludes its work, needed reforms of the Gun Control Act of 1968 will have been made while legitimate law enforcement concerns have been protected.

PRO

by Hon. JAMES A. McCLURE
United States Senator, Idaho, Republican

From the debate of June 24, 1985, on the floor of the U.S. Senate during consideration of S. 49, the proposed Federal Firearms Owners' Protection Act.

All too often we in the legislative branch have a short attention span. We see a problem; we pass a law—and then we forget the whole thing.

When Congress enacted the Gun Control Act of 1968, it intended to curb violent firearms crime by controlling the sale, transportation, and possession of guns. Did this approach work? No. It did not. Extensive hearings and study of the actual enforcement of this law clearly show that the ones who bear the brunt of this law are not necessarily the most dangerous criminals. The ones who have been harassed by the enforcement of this act are often innocent men and women who have bungled their paperwork. Punishment has been swift and severe. While genuine criminals are all too often let free to roam the streets, these law-abiding gun owners and dealers have had their property unconstitutionally seized and held and their businesses and lives ruined. People who have done their best to comply with the law are forced to bear the stigma of Federal felons.

We have a duty to provide for the legal protection of the citizens of this country, and when the force of the law is directed at the innocent, and does nothing to the guilty, we are neglecting that duty.

It has been said that fanaticism is redoubling your efforts when you have lost sight of your goals. I believe the Firearm Owners' Protection Act will bring Federal firearms law closer to the intent of Congress—directing enforcement effort away from insignificant paperwork errors and toward willful violations of Federal firearms law.

My colleagues on the Judiciary Committee worked long and hard during past Congresses, as I did, to hammer out changes in the law that will prevent the abuses we have seen. This law touches on many people, on many branches of the Government. We have labored to balance the need for effective law enforcement with the right of honest citizens to constitutional protections. We have all spent time ironing out our differences on this complicated and emotionally charged issue. I do not suppose there is a comma or a parenthesis that has escaped discussion.

At length, we arrived at a compromise that solved the major problems. I have met with representatives from different groups in the firearms rights community, and I believe that we now have a piece of legislation that everyone can honestly support. The bill was voted out of committee—unanimously. And, with two exceptions, that bill, as voted by the committee, is before us today.

The Firearm Owners' Protection Act is designed to correct demonstrated abuses in present law. It would make the following reforms:

Define "engaging in the business" to clarify who needs a Federal firearms license; liberalize the interstate sale of firearms when these sales are legal in both State of sale, and State of purchase; mandate an element of criminal intention for prosecution and conviction of Federal firearms law violations; clarify procedures for dealer sales of firearms from his private collection; permit inspection of dealer's records for reasonable cause; require mandatory penalties for the use of a firearm during a Federal crime; limit seizure of firearms; provide for the return of seized firearms, and grant attorney's fees in spiteful or frivolous suits; and allow the interstate transportation of unloaded, inaccessible firearms.

The bill would not do the following: Allow mail order sales of firearms; allow unlicensed pawn shop gun sales and restrict legitimate inspection of records.

In short, this bill—which this entire body now has a chance to consider, has been painstakingly crafted to focus law enforcement on the kinds of Federal firearms law violations most likely to contribute to violent firearms crime. Enactment of this bill into law will insure that the intent of Congress is carried out.

We must compel the enforcing agency to stop harassing honest people and to direct their efforts at the violent criminals who give all gun owners a bad name. This can only be done by changing present Federal firearms law. We must change that law.

We must draft laws that secure safety for our citizens, but when a well meant law—the Gun Control Act of 1968—does the very opposite, when it practically guarantees that the constitutional rights of ordinary, law-abiding people will be violated, we must change that law. It is a bad law. Its intentions are good, but a bad law. We have an opportunity now, with the Firearm Owners' Protection Act, to correct the mistakes of the past.

I made reference to the fact that there are two changes in the bill from that which was reported out by the Judiciary Committee. One was with respect to the restrictions on a sale in a State where it is lawful to sell a firearm to a nonresident of that State as it deals with respect to what Senator Kennedy and others have described as snubbies. The other change in the law, as reported by the Judiciary Committee, is to leave out the so-called cop-killer bullet provision that was passed and was contained in that bill at that time; because the Senate has since that time passed another provision, it was felt unnecessary to repeat that provision of the bill as reported by the Judiciary Committee.

I am delighted that the Senate, at long last, will have an opportunity to work its will with respect to the provisions of the bill and the amendment of the 1968 Firearms Act, which I think was misdirected, and to redirect that in proper channels.

CON
by Hon. CHARLES McC. MATHIAS
United States Senator, Maryland, Republican

From the debate of June 9, 1985, on the floor of the U.S. Senate during consideration of S. 49, the pending Federal Firearms Owners' Protection Act. Sen. Mathias was the author of a proposed amendment seeking to eliminate advance notice of compliance inspections of firearms dealers.

The issue of gun control involves strong, often conflicting interests that need to be considered and weighed carefully. On the other hand, I can well understand many of our citizens' concern for self-defense at a time of unacceptably high crime rates, as well as the need to protect the legitimate rights of sportsmen. At the same time, I am aware of the obvious need for protection against the lawless use of easily obtainable and concealable handguns that all too often are used in the commission of violent crimes.

As a Member of Congress for the past 25 years, I have tried to help shape a coherent, fair and effective Federal policy in this sensitive area to advance the effort to curb violent crime, without imposing unduly burdensome and bureaucratic procedures on law-abiding Americans.

After careful study, I have concluded that the enactment of S. 49 would be a step away from this goal. Therefore, I shall vote against this bill.

S. 49 would unnecessarily tilt the balance against local law enforcement officials and local crime prevention efforts. At the same time, this bill offers very little benefit to the sportsman and no benefit whatever to the citizen who possesses a gun for personal defense in the home.

Since I was first elected to Congress, I have consistently opposed legislation to require the registration of firearms owners, or to ban the possession of handguns by law-abiding citizens. I shall continue to oppose such proposals. But those issues have nothing to do with the legislation that is before us today.

prohibition of interstate sales of handguns. It would be practically impossible for a dealer to determine that sales to out-of-State purchasers conform to the applicable State or local laws which are in a constant state of flux and whose application may vary greatly according to individual State court decisions.

The Senate Judiciary Committee, when considering similar legislation in 1984, recognized that the interstate sale of handguns could jeopardize State and local law enforcement and added language to the bill to retain the restrictions on interstate sales for handguns with barrel lengths of less than 3 inches, the so-called snubbies. S. 49 does not contain this important Judiciary Committee amendment.

Another weakening provision of S. 49 would require advance notice to gun dealers before compliance inspections. At present, agents of the Bureau of Alcohol, Tobacco, and Firearms (BATF) are authorized to conduct surprise visits to inspect sales records maintained by federally licensed gun dealers. S. 49 would require that a dealer be given reasonable notice before an inspection. With less than 100 BATF agents and over 200,000 handgun dealers in this country, unannounced visits are necessary, if inspection is to serve as a deterrent and be effective in ensuring that weapons are distributed through lawful channels in a traceable manner, that sales to undesirable customers are prevented, and the origin of particular firearms are detected.

An amendment to be offered by the senior Senator from Maryland would retain current law with respect to surprise Federal compliance inspections and should be supported.

Another amendment for which I urge support and acceptance is the provision which would require a 14-day waiting period between the time of negotiation for sale of a handgun and its time of delivery. This amendment would not mandate a criminal background check on the purchaser; rather, it would allow State and local authorities to exercise that option. It would also provide an exception from the waiting period for purchasers who present a notarized statement from the local police chief stating that immediate possession of the handgun is necessary for the individual's personal safety.

Such a waiting period, which was recommended by the 1981 Attorney General's Task Force on Violent Crime and which has broad support among the law enforcement community, will go a long way to facilitate background checks to keep handguns out of the wrong hands. It would also serve as a cooling off period for those intent on suicide or crimes of passion. I have supported a waiting period for handgun purchases during consideration of earlier legislation relating to handguns, and I would remind my colleagues that an identical provision was adopted by the Senate Judiciary Committee during markup of similar legislation in 1982.

I am convinced that these amendments to S. 49, which I have discussed briefly, are essential improvements which would enhance law enforcement and prevent handguns from falling into the wrong hands. They would not place undue restrictions on honest citizens with respect to the acquisition, possession, or use of firearms for recreational or other lawful purposes. I strongly urge my colleagues to approve these amendments which will be offered during consideration of S. 49. Without these amendments, the bill should not be passed.

PRO
by Hon. ORRIN G. HATCH
United States Senator, Utah, Republican

From the debate of June 24, 1985, on the floor of the U.S. Senate during consideration of S. 49, the pending Federal Firearms Owners' Protection Act. Sen. Hatch served as majority floor manager of the bill during the debate.

The opening of this debate culminates a lengthy legislative process to ensure greater protection for the constitutional rights of firearm owners. S. 49 deregulates the acquisition, possession, and use of firearms for lawful purposes and redirects Federal firearm enforcement toward criminal violators. Thus, S. 49 reaffirms the stated intent of the 1968 Gun Control Act to avoid "any undue or unnecessary Federal restrictions or burdens on law-abiding citizens." Despite this stated intent of the Gun Control Act, numerous hearings have revealed that the 1968 act has failed to strike an appropriate balance between the constitutional rights of law-abiding gun owners and law enforcement interests.

Rather than focusing on violent crime, Federal firearm enforcement instead has become mired down in enforcing minor technical infractions. Inadvertent recordkeeping errors have given rise to major felony prosecutions. An occasional sale from a dealer's private collection has resulted in felony charges. Warrantless searches have unnecessarily harassed law-abiding firearms dealers. The absence of any definitions for "engaging in the business" have subjected casual hobbyists or collectors to prosecution for dealing in firearms without a license. The absence of any criminal state of mind requirements—*mens rea*—for felony violations have resulted in severe penalties for unintentional infractions of technical rules. Requirements for recordkeeping on ammunition have imposed enormous burdens on firearm dealers which were not needed for adequate law enforcement. This list could be expanded. In general, the 1968 act needs modification to eliminate some unintended consequences of its broad or unclear language.

Permit me to rehearse for you the liberty that the Framers considered important enough to list second in the Constitution, immediately following the freedoms of speech and religion:

"A well regulated militia being necessary to the security of a free state, the right of the people to keep and bear arms shall not be infringed."

The language of the amendment itself explains why the Framers considered this right important enough to list second. They thought the "security of a free state" would depend on the right to keep and bear arms.

Like so many of our basic liberties, the right to keep and bear arms may be traced to common law origins in England even before America was settled. The English Bill of Rights of 1689 contained the right to "have arms." The famed English jurist Blackstone listed in his Commentaries the "right of having and using arms for self-preservation and defense." This right is literally older than the constitution itself. In fact, if our forefathers had not exercised this right at Lexington and Concord, we may never have had a constitution.

In America, the Revolutionary War was hastened by the King's attempt to disarm the colonists. Outraged at the King's gun controls, our own hot-blooded patriot, Patrick Henry, in his "give me liberty" speech feared the colonists would wait too long to take up arms. He exclaimed: "Will it be when we are totally disarmed? . . . Three million people armed in the holy cause of liberty are invincible." Indeed, the "shot heard round the world" at Lexington and Concord was the result of General Gage's attempt to seize some ammunition and firearms. In one sense the Revolutionary War was the first gun control fight. We won that gun control battle.

After the war, on September 17, 1787, 39 men gathered in Philadelphia to culminate 16 hot weeks of summer work by signing the Constitution. The process did not end there, however. Article VII required the ratification of three-quarters of the States. Three delegates, including the powerful George Mason of Virginia, refused to sign the document because it lacked a Bill of Rights.

Without a Bill of Rights, the Constitution came under immediate attack. One zealous opponent protested that under the Constitution, Congress "at their pleasure may arm or disarm all or any part of the freemen of the United States." If he was upset then, imagine how he would react today to the 1968 Gun Control Act.

Let us examine the subtle attempts of some courts and politicians to drain the meaning out of the second amendment. Their first line of attack is to contend that "the right of the people to keep and bear arms" is merely a collective right referring to the people collectively as a common body instead of as individual citizens. In other words, they would say, the amendment only prohibits Federal interference with State National Guard weaponry.

This faulty reading of the amendment simply does not square with the history of the Bill of Rights. When the Senate considered the second amendment in 1789, it specifically rejected a motion on the floor that would have limited the right to bearing arms only "for the common defense." The authors of the amendment wanted no such restrictions.

The notion of limiting the second amendment by undue emphasis on the militia language also breaks down for another reason. In 1972, Congress enacted the Militia Act making all able-bodied men between 18–45 members of the militia. Indeed, the current United States Code still, by law, defines the militia as "all able-bodied males" between 17 and 45. The "militia" mentioned in the amendment is not limited to the State National Guard. The patriots at Lexington, though just a gathering of freedom-loving farmers, was a militia. The second amendment's "militia" is the "whole body of the people." In fact, its very language says it is a "right of the people."

Finally, it is important to remember that the first and fourth amendments also use the language "right of the people." Clearly those amendments—approved at the same time as the second amendment—grant individual rights to peaceably assemble and to be free of arbitrary searches. Likewise, keeping and bearing arms is an individual right. In fact, as Justice Story of the Supreme Court once said, the right to keep and bear arms is the "palladium [protector] of the liberties of the Republic." It is the means of preserving the other rights.

The other attack on the second amendment is even more insidious than misleading doubts about the meaning of the language. You are familiar with these efforts to undermine our right. This attack suggests that guns, instead of criminals, are responsible for violent crime.

It is difficult to understand, based on the foregoing evidence, how a right so fundamental as the individual right to bear arms could be misunderstood today. It was obviously well understood at the time of the adoption of the Bill of Rights and for decades thereafter. According to a recent public opinion poll, 88 percent of Americans today still believe in the individual right to keep and bear arms. I am talking about the 1978 Decision Making Information polls. The history of the second amendment and what it stands for is clear. The people of our Nation overwhelmingly support this right, which is so fundamental to our freedoms and liberties as Americans.

Despite the intent of Congress when the Bill of Rights was adopted, the second amendment has been under attack. Many well-meaning citizens and lawmakers, appropriately appalled at escalating levels of crime, have drawn the mistaken conclusion that guns, instead of criminals, are responsible for violence. While I do not underestimate the seriousness of our violent crime plague, I state categorically that the solution to this crime epidemic is not to take firearms away from law-abiding citizens. Blaming guns for a criminal's violence makes no more sense than blaming automobiles for drunk drivers. Moreover, outlawing guns to stop crime makes no more sense than does outlawing cars to stop drunk driving.

Crime statistics make clear that gun control is not crime control. Legislation that regulates the use and availability of firearms, including handguns, does not reduce crime. Studies show that cities and States with restrictive gun control laws have higher crime rates than areas with less restrictive laws concerning guns. Handgun availability, based on handguns in circulation per 100,000 population, has increased over 90 percent in the past 15 years. However, handgun involvement in homicide has fallen from a reported 48 percent in 1967 to 43.5 percent in 1982. Firearm ownership overall has increased almost 60 percent and yet gun involvement in homicide has fallen. The highest homicide and other violent crime rates remain in gun-restrictive areas—New York City had more homicides than the combined total of 23 States with a population of 37 million had covering half the land area of the United States. With a virtual handgun ban, Washington, D.C. has become the most violent large city in the Nation. Firearms involvement in violent crime in Washington, D.C. is increasing—while decreasing nationally and in big cities in general. Massachusetts, with a restrictive gun control law, continues to watch violent crime rise at a rate twice that of the rest of the country.

In November 1981, the Justice Department released the Executive Summary and Literature Review of the massive study of Weapons, Crime, and Violence in America. The research conducted primarily by Professors James Wright and Peter Rossi of the University of Massachusetts at Amherst reviewed literature and studies to determine what definitive evidence exists on issues relating to weapons, violence, and crime. It examined the amount and quality of criminal justice data available on weapons through a national survey of 609 law enforcement agencies and an analysis of court records of a sample of 5,000 felony cases processed by the Los Angeles Superior Court. In short, the research proved exhaustive, and its findings were unequivocal. The researchers concluded that "there is little evidence to show that gun ownership among the population as a whole is, per se, an important cause of criminal violence," and there is no conclusive evidence that restrictive gun laws—Federal, State, or local—either impair the access of criminals to firearms or reduce the amount of violent crime.

Professors Wright and Rossi found that many of the common assumptions about the firearms and crime issue are unsupported. They found that 50 percent of American families acknowledge gun ownership and that three-fourths of these privately owned guns are used for sport and recreation; the remainder for self-defense. They found no persuasive evidence to support the allegation that most homicide would not occur were firearms generally less available. And they concluded that "any action taken to deny firearms to would-be criminals will necessarily deny them to a vastly larger group of persons who will never contemplate, much less commit, a violent criminal act"—a cost which must be "weighed against the anticipated benefits before a rational policy decision can be made."

The cost to which these researchers alluded is two-fold: The cost to life and the cost to civil rights and civil liberties.

They found that privately owned handguns seem to be about as effective a deterrent to crime as is the legal system. Between 2 and 6 percent of the adult population has actually fired a gun in self-defense.

Using guns for protection reduces the chance that violent crime will be successfully completed.

On the basis of this evidence it is clear that any gun control, such as limitation and/or registration, works mainly to regulate many law-abiding citizens who do not use their weapons for violent purposes, but for sport, self-defense, and collecting. Law enforcement officials spend many wasted hours regulating honest citizens, hours that could be spent cutting down crime.

This and other evidence shows not only that gun control laws do not have their desired and intended effect, but that gun control restrictions actually increase the incidence of violent crime and homicide. If we are to be successful in reducing this crime, we must attack it directly. Efforts to curb our constitutional freedom to bear arms, while possibly well-intended, are misdirected and counterproductive.

The Gun Control Act of 1968 permits the Government to charge persons with inadvertent offenses, confiscate weapons based on agent opinions as to their future use, and so forth. Yet it provides no restitution to the victim of these practices, even when they are misused for oppression. In many cases where the individual secures vindication, he does so only at the price of financial ruin—or winds up letting guns be illegally kept because he cannot afford to hire an attorney to challenge the confiscation. The Reform Act would permit a judge to award attorney's fees to the citizen in a gun confiscation case if the citizen wins the return of the firearms, or in any other proceeding, if the judge finds that the Agency proceeded in an oppressive way or acted in bad faith.

It is unthinkable that such injustices should be allowed to continue, fostered by the law of the land. Change is needed, and S. 49 will provide the necessary alteration.

CON
by Hon. CARL M. LEVIN
United States Senator, Michigan, Democrat

From the debate of July 9, 1985, on the floor of the U.S. Senate during consideration of S. 49, the pending Federal Firearms Owners' Protection Act.

I will vote against S. 49 because it increases the burdens on law enforcement officials in protecting Americans from crimes committed with "Saturday night specials." I support the desire of proponents of S. 49 to eliminate or modify provisions in the 1968 law which place unreasonable or unfair regulatory requirements on dealers and on owners of guns.

However, in the final analysis the bill will make it easier for individuals to cross State lines, often in order to avoid laws of their own States, to purchase "Saturday night specials," which have no legitimate sporting purpose.

I can understand the desire of the Congress to ease excessive burdens on legitimate gun dealers. I can understand the Congress desiring to remove unnecessary impediments on the sale of rifles and long guns. But what I cannot understand is why the Congress would seek to increase the burdens on law enforcement officials by increasing the possibility that criminals will obtain "Saturday night specials"—for which there is only one clear purpose—a criminal purpose.

Members of the law enforcement community shared this concern. That is why they strongly supported the amendment offered by Senator Kennedy which would have retained the existing ban on interstate sales of handguns. The International Association of Police Chiefs, the Fraternal Order of Police, and the National Black Law Enforcement Executives wrote to Members of Congress urging that current restrictions on the interstate sale of handguns be retained. According to one chief of police, lifting the current restrictions " . . . would have a devastating effect on law enforcement efforts."

The easing of these restrictions was made all the more unacceptable by the defeat of the amendment which would have provided for a 14-day waiting period for those who would purchase handguns. The waiting period was endorsed by many law enforcement organizations.

It is intended to keep handguns out of the hands of persons with records of violence or drug use.

We need to assist law enforcement officers in their effort to reduce crime. That is why I am opposing this legislation.

CON
by Hon. CHRISTOPHER J. DODD
United States Senator, Connecticut, Democrat

From the debate of July 9, 1985, on the floor of the U.S. Senate during consideration of S. 49, the pending Federal Firearms Owners' Protection Act.

I rise in strong opposition to this legislation in its present form. While I have many concerns with the bill before the Senate, I believe it is still possible, with the approval of certain crucial amendments, to enact a responsible bill.

This legislation, as proposed, turns back the clock of Federal protection against handgun crime in seeking to overturn key provisions of the modest Gun Control Act of 1968, as passed in the wake of the assassinations of Martin Luther King, Jr., and Robert F. Kennedy. This measure would weaken our national firearms laws and effectively take, as the National Rifle Association has called it, "the first step toward repealing the 1968 Gun Control Act."

The Gun Control Act of 1968 was intended to keep handguns out of the wrong hands—the felon, the minor, the unlawful drug user, the mental incompetent—and to punish harshly those who use handguns in crime. The centerpiece of the act is the broad prohibition of interstate commerce in firearms by unlicensed, private citizens. The legislation we consider here today eliminates that prohibition, allowing once again easy mail access to guns by criminals and would-be assassins.

My father, the late Senator Thomas Dodd, dedicated much of his Senate service to putting an end to such easy availability of firearms to criminals. He was chairman of the Senate's Juvenile Delinquency Subcommittee, where he conducted numerous hearings in the 1960's on the unrestricted availability of firearms. My father was astounded by what he discovered. Bazookas, handguns, and an assortment of automatic weapons were on display in his subcommittee—the undeniable and frightening evidence of the ease with which these lethal weapons could be acquired—at times even by the children of committee staff.

My father led an uphill and oftentimes exasperating battle to move legislation aimed at keeping guns out of the hands of criminals through the full committee and onto the Senate floor. He never lost faith, and I am proud to say, remained a driving force behind final passage of the Gun Control Act of 1968. He refused to believe that the gun runners, the hoodlums, the crackpots, and the self-styled vigilantes were more powerful than the American people. My father believed in his own words, that "the American people will not forget the assassination of President Kennedy with a weapon fraudulently obtained through the mails, nor could they forget the other needless tragedies that they read about every day."

I refuse to believe that our national nightmare over the assassination of President Kennedy has been forgotten.

It would be disconcerting, indeed, for this body to repeal the very provision whose purpose is to prevent such tragedy.

Another concern I have with this bill is that it was placed directly on the Senate Calendar, by-passing the careful scrutiny of the Senate Judiciary Committee. I believe it was a mistake to reintroduce the bill this year without the compromises that painstakingly were worked out by the Judiciary Committee last year to prohibit the interstate sale of "snubbies"—handguns with barrel lengths less than 3 inches. It has been well documented that 11 to 15 handguns most often used in the commission of murder, armed robbery, and other street crimes had snub-nosed barrels of 2.5 inches or less. Criminals favor concealability. Short barrels mean inaccuracy at anything beyond point blank range. They should therefore be of little interest to legitimate hunters, hobbyists, and target-shooters.

I also would have liked to have seen a waiting period included in this bill, a provision adopted by the Senate Judiciary Committee in the 98th Congress. The Gun Control Act of 1968, while setting forth categories of persons to whom firearms may not be sold, does not require verification of the purchaser's eligibility. A person purchasing a firearm from a federally licensed dealer is only required to sign a form on which he affirms by sworn statement that he is not proscribed from purchasing a firearm. As one might expect, this "honor system" of verification has done little to prevent proscribed persons from obtaining firearms.

The 1981 Attorney General's Task Force on Violent Crime addressed this loophole in Federal gun laws and recommended that "a waiting period be required for the purchase of a handgun to allow for a mandatory records check to ensure that the purchaser is not one of the categories of persons who are proscribed by existing Federal law from receiving a handgun." A number of States and municipalities, including my home State of Connecticut, have enacted waiting period laws which have proven to be effective in keeping handguns out of the wrong hands.

The idea of a waiting period has broad public support. The law enforcement community, including the International Association of Chiefs of Police and the National Association of Attorneys General, supports a waiting period for handgun purchases. Moreover, a 1981 Gallup poll showed that 91 percent of the American people support a 21-day waiting period for handgun purchases with a background check.

I am also concerned that this legislation would, in its present form, preempt Connecticut's restrictions on automobile transportation of a firearm without a license, clearly an intrinsic part of my home State's license-to-carry law. This represents a derogation of the rights of States to regulate firearms within their own borders, a policy contrary to the intent of the Gun Control Act of 1968. I believe this goes too far. The interstate transportation of hunting rifles and shotguns does not pose the same law enforcement problem that the transportation of handguns does. In my view, an amendment to the bill could meet the needs of both hunters and law enforcement by restricting the provision allowing interstate transportation to long guns.

I have a number of other concerns with this bill, but in the interest of time, I will reserve my comments for the present. I am sure some of my colleagues will be addressing these same concerns as we move forward on this legislation.

Finally, I would urge my colleagues to give serious thought to what is being asked of us here. We are being asked to relax and weaken our already modest Federal protections against handgun crime. In effect, we are being asked to further hinder the ability of law enforcement officers to respond to violent crime. More than 10,000 Americans will be murdered with handguns this year. If we add up the number of Americans killed just with handguns since 1968, the total is a staggering 350,000. Surely, the time has not come to loosen Federal restrictions on criminals' access to handguns.

I urge my colleagues to vote against this bill in its present form.

PRO
by Hon. ROBERT KASTEN
United States Senator, Wisconsin, Republican

From the debate of July 9, 1985, on the floor of the U.S. Senate during consideration of S. 49, the pending Federal Firearms Owners' Protection Act.

The Firearm Owners' Protection Act was conceived in the notion that law enforcement needed to be directed at the real criminals, not someone who makes an honest mistake in his bookkeeping. It was obvious that the hastily enacted Gun Control Act of 1968, which Senator McClure's bill refines, made it easy for over-zealous agents of the Bureau of Alcohol, Tobacco, and Firearms to spend a lot of enforcement effort snooping out violations so far removed from the general notion of gun crime that it would be funny, if the result were not so tragic.

The sponsors and proponents of the Gun Control Act of 1968 claimed that it would significantly reduce the rate of crime, particularly crimes involving the use of firearms. It has not. Instead, between 1967 and 1982, the national homicide and handgun-homicide rates rose 50 percent, while robbery rates and robberies involving the use of firearms have nearly tripled. Clearly, the 1968 act has served to reduce neither the rate of violent crime nor the use of firearms in the commission of crime. It has, however, increased the regulatory burden imposed on law-abiding American citizens—gun owners and dealers—and subjected those same citizens to the threat of severe penalties for technical violations of the law caused by inadvertent errors. We saw this clearly in a long series of hearings.

Every point in the Firearm Owners' Protection Act is designed to correct a documented problem. Every point is aimed at directing law enforcement toward those violations of Federal firearms law that are most likely to contribute to violent firearms crime—those who knowingly sell to prohibited persons, those who knowingly traffic in stolen firearms. It's just not cost effective to allow law enforcement to follow its old pattern of snooping after minor paperwork errors.

Today, nearly half the households in America own some kind of firearm: estimates suggest that private citizens in this country own between 120 and 140 million guns. These people are not criminals. They are decent, responsible men and women, union members, business executives, doctors, lawyers, teachers, civil servants, elected officials—including a number of U.S. Senators and Representatives, and others too numerous to mention. Their guns are purchased for hunting, sporting activities, collecting, self-defense, and other legal purposes. These American citizens should not be the victims of Federal agents seeking to administer Federal law.

Yet, my colleagues in this body should be aware that the Senate Subcommittee on the Constitution has found that 75 percent of Federal firearms prosecutions are aimed at ordinary citizens who had neither criminal intent nor any knowledge they were breaking the law. The Gun Control Act of 1968 allows the unreasonable and unwarranted infringement of rights guaranteed to all Americans under the second amendment to the Constitution. It is an intolerable situation which we must act to correct.

Federal firearms law is a complicated matter. Fine-tuning this portion of Federal law is no simple matter. Jim McClure has worked long and hard to come up with corrections that answer every objection. I think he has succeeded—this legislation was voted out of the Judiciary Committee unanimously. I urge my colleagues to follow the committee's lead and cast their votes for this bill, for the right of the American citizen to keep and bear arms, and, untimately, for the protection of our Constitution.

CON
by Hon. JOHN F. KERRY
United States Senator, Massachusetts, Democrat

From the debate of July 9, 1985, on the floor of the U.S. Senate during consideration of S. 49, the pending Federal Firearms Owners' Protection Act.

As we consider S. 49, the McClure-Volkmer Firearms Owners' Protection Act, I think it is useful to recall the history of the legislation this act is to modify—the Gun Control Act of 1968, passed in the wake of the assassinations of Martin Luther King and Robert Kennedy by men using handguns.

Sadly, it took these two assassinations to convince Congress after 5 years of debate to pass basic regulations on the interstate sale of firearms. The act was designed to "provide support to Federal, State, and local law enforcement officials in their fight against crime and violence." Its passage was in recognition of the fact that gun violence in the United States had grown to alarming proportions. The legislative history of the act shows that one of the principal purposes of the legislation was to provide aid to the States against the "migratory handgun."

A major aim of the Gun Control Act was to assist State and local gun control efforts by reducing the flow of guns from loose-control to tight-control jurisdictions. Prior to the act, two Northeastern States, including my home State of Massachusetts, and a number of municipalities had attempted to restrict handgun possession to only those of their citizens who could demonstrate a special need to own one.

Such laws were intended to reduce handgun ownership to a tiny fraction of the national average of 40 handguns per 100 households. As it turned out, municipal efforts to restrict handgun possession were vulnerable to the flow of handguns from within the States and from other States. And even State efforts were vulnerable to interstate traffic.

A major problem in administering any gun licensing system was the interstate "leakage" of guns. In the mid-1960's, it was estimated that 87 percent of all firearms used in Massachusetts crime had been purchased first in other States. Two-thirds of a sample of handguns confiscated in New York City had come from other States, and surveys in other States told the same story.

It was to meet this problem directly that the 1968 statute was enacted—to stop the frustration of local efforts to license and register ownership of guns.

The centerpiece of the new regulatory scheme was the ban on interstate shipments to or from persons who do not possess Federal licenses as dealers, manufacturers, importers or collectors, coupled with the declaration that it was unlawful for any person other than a Federal license holder to engage in the business of manufacturing or dealing in firearms. The act thus granted Federal licensees a monopoly on interstate transactions and required a Federal license to engage in any but isolated intrastate transactions.

While private citizens were to be excluded from commerce in guns, federally licensed dealers were to be much more strenuously regulated. The fees from all Federal licenses were increased. Minimum standards for licensees were set, and the Secretary of the Treasury was given broad powers to establish mechanisms for regulating licensed manufacturers and dealers.

Having established Federal regulation of those in the business of making, selling and importing firearms, as well as all interstate aspects of commerce in firearms, the act pursued its major aims with a series of criminal prohibitions.

Those without Federal licenses were prohibited from shipping guns to other private parties in another State and from transferring guns to persons they knew or had reason to believe were residents of another State.

Dealers were prohibited from shipping to private citizens in other States and from selling to those who the dealer knew or had reason to believe resided out of State.

All dealers had to sign a form indicating a customer had produced identification showing he was not a resident of another State. This form, which also identified the firearms sold and gave the purchaser's name, address, and description was retained by the dealer and made available for inspection by Alcohol, Tobacco and Firearms agents.

All of this provided a Federal framework for the monitoring of interstate firearms sales to help State and local efforts to keep arms away from criminals, and to trace weapons when they were used to commit crimes. This Federal regulatory system was the heart and soul of the 1968 Gun Control Act. And yet, the McClure-Volkmer bill, without the amendments we have had placed before us today, will substantially dismantle this regulatory system, and again make it extraordinarily difficult for localities and States to fight crime committed with guns.

For these reasons, I offer my strong support to the amendment offered by Senator Kennedy to maintain the current interstate sales regulations of handguns. Those of us who were in law enforcement at the local level know that local efforts to monitor and track weapons will be made practically impossible if the Kennedy amendment is not adopted to maintain existing law in this area.

Senator Kennedy has worked tirelessly on behalf of all those injured by criminals with guns or who lost friends or family through crimes or abuse of firearms, and on behalf of law enforcement officials, to make the McClure-Volkmer legislation protect them, as well as gun owners.

I strongly urge this body to adopt the Kennedy amendment.

I am aware of the concerns of law-abiding firearms owners and recognize that McClure-Volkmer may eliminate some unintended consequences of the 1968 law. But law-abiding firearms owners will not be hurt by amendments to this legislation such as the Mathias amendment, which eliminates notification to dealers before Federal compliance inspections. I think it is incredible that a Federal agency trying to make sure that the law is followed should have to give a dealer notice before an inspection, to give him time to get his house in order if he has been violating the law. This notification provision does nothing to help those who are law-abiding—it only protects those who are violating the law, by interfering with law enforcement.

PRO
by Hon. Steven D. Symms
United States Senator, Idaho, Republican

From the Senate floor debate of July 9, 1985, during consideration of S. 49, the proposed Federal Firearms Owners' Protection Act.

I rise in support of S. 49, a bill to protect the constitutional rights, civil liberties, and rights to privacy of firearm owners.

Our proper goal in considering any legislation affecting the public's access to, and use of, firearms is clear. We must aim at striking a careful balance, between the rights of law-abiding citizens on the one hand, and the pressing need for effective law enforcement on the other. I believe S. 49, as amended, meets this test.

S. 49 makes several useful changes in the scope of Federal regulations affecting firearms. These changes both protect the rights of individual gun owners and aid law enforcement, by making it clear that gun owners who only occasionally sell or repair firearms, or who sell all or part of their collections will not have to go through the cumbersome, time-consuming process of obtaining a Federal license. These changes will allow the Bureau of Alcohol, Tobacco, and Firearms to concentrate its scarce resources on those businesses who handle most of the gun trade.

Another important change in current law made by S. 49 would permit individuals to mail legally owned firearms to a licensed manufacturer, importer, or dealer for repair, customization, or other lawful purpose. This change could not allow mail order sales of firearms by licensees to nonlicensees. Instead, it would remove an unnecessary and awkward impediment to legitimate commerce.

S. 49 also removes another needless barrier to commerce by permitting face-to-face sales by licensees to persons who do not reside in the licensees' State, so long as the sales are legal in the respective States of both the buyer and seller. This eliminates the need for a collector, hunter, or other law-abiding citizen to go through the very complicated procedures required by current law for acquiring a rare or customized firearm from a licensed dealer in another State.

Finally, this bill clarifies existing law to allow the Treasury Department to revoke firearms licenses only in the case of willful violations of law. This clarification represents a recognition that the paperwork required by the 1968 Gun Control Act is exceedingly complex; even the best-intentioned gun dealers are liable to make inadvertent, technical mistakes. The need for effective and appropriate law enforcement dictates that the Government not spend scarce resources prosecuting honest citizens who make mistakes, but the minority who operate in disregard of the law.

I have never believed that the rights of gun owners and the Government's responsibility to enforce the law necessarily need to be in conflict. S. 49, by removing many unnecessary restrictions on the lawful activities of honest citizens, protects individual rights guaranteed in the Constitution. I believe that S. 49 does this without jeopardizing the Government's ability to combat crime—by more carefully targeting the thrust of the 1968 Gun Control Act, S. 49 enhances the Government's capacity to go after criminals. I urge my colleagues to approve this important legislation.

UNDER THE GUN[8]

"This is a momentous day for American gun owners," a spokesman for the National Rifle Association declared recently. The NRA had cause to celebrate. It has worked for 17 years to overturn the Gun Control Act, and on July 9 that goal seemed almost within reach. The Senate had voted, 79 to 15, to loosen restrictions on firearms dealers and to make it easier for people to buy and transport lethal weapons.

The success of the McClure-Volkmer bill, sponsored by Republican Senator James A. McClure of Idaho and Democratic Representative Harold L. Volkmer of Missouri, took many Americans by surprise. Twenty-two years ago this November, Lee Harvey Oswald assassinated President Kennedy with a rifle bought by mail order from an advertisement in the National Rifle Association's magazine. Five years later, Martin Luther King Jr. was gunned down outside his Memphis motel room, and Sirhan Sirhan shot Robert Kennedy with a .22 caliber pistol as he left a campaign rally in Los Angeles. In the years since the passage of the Gun Control Act in 1968, a majority of the population has favored even stricter handgun controls.

But the NRA wasn't surprised. It had been shrewd in its choice of political allies, and in its lobbying tactics. In 1983-84, it contributed a total of $95,000 to the campaigns of senators who wound up voting for the bill, and spent $423,000 on bumper stickers, bill boards, and radio ads to get them elected. As the Senate vote approached, handgun lobbying groups began sending off letters to senators. "The eyes of 80 million law-abiding firearm owners are focused on you," the Citizens' Right to Keep and Bear Arms Committee ominously warned. On the day the bill came up in the Senate, the NRA sent around a letter claiming that the National Sheriffs' Association supported it. In fact, like most police organizations around the country, the Sheriffs' Association vehemently opposed it. The bill was rushed to a vote only 12 working days after it was announced, while the media were preoccupied with the hostage crisis and the Fourth of July. No hearings were held.

[8]Editorial. Reprinted by permission from *New Republic*, Ag. 26, '85, pp. 7-8. Copyright © 1985 by *New Republic*.

Supporters of the legislation see it as a vindication of the rights of legitimate gun users who have been unfairly penalized by the Gun Control Act. Its sponsors cite cases of hunters and sportsmen who are charged with a felony if they stray into a neighboring state with an unloaded rifle in their car trunk. And they point out that firearms dealers risk five years in jail if they do not keep accurate sales records. The bill would relax these rules and make it easier for legitimate gun users to buy, sell, and transport firearms.

It would also erode the basis of the Gun Control Act. The only way to limit gun-related crime, as Congress realized in 1968, is to place a sometimes burdensome responsibility on law-abiding gun owners and dealers. They are the only ones, after all, who can ensure that their guns do not end up in the hands of criminals. The McClure-Volkmer bill would allow gun owners the freedom to be careless or irresponsible. Dealers could sell guns from their "personal collections" without keeping any records, and those who broke the law could escape punishment by pleading ignorance. Regardless of local laws, owners would be permitted to transport pistols—as well as sporting rifles—across state lines as long as they were not loaded and "not readily accessible." A would-be assassin could legally carry an unloaded handgun right to the White House gates.

What's more, the bill would take all the deterrent force out of federal inspections. At present, the Bureau of Alcohol, Tobacco and Firearms can inspect a gun dealer's records unannounced as often as it feels necessary. The McClure-Volkmer bill would limit the ATF to one visit per year, and dealers would have to be given advance notice. This makes about as much sense as putting up warning signs on a freeway a mile before every speed trap. The purpose of inspections is to make gun traders abide by the law even when a federal agent is *not* expected. As Senator Edward Kennedy pointed out, surprise inspections are permitted to guarantee that mines are operated safely, and that prescription drugs are correctly dispensed. Why not also to prevent the sale of handguns to felons?

These loopholes were not left open by mistake. Early in the debate, Senator Kennedy proposed an amendment to ease regulations on hunting and sporting rifles while retaining them for handguns. Only a handful of senators turned up to hear his speech; 69 voted against the amendment. Senator Charles McC.

Mathias then introduced an amendment to allow surprise inspections of firearms dealers. It too was firmly rejected.

A life member of the NRA, President Reagan has made no secret of his support for the bill. Indeed, it is an opportune way to appease his conservative supporters, disgruntled by the Supreme Court's moderation on abortion and school prayer. Yet handgun decontrol sits somewhat uneasily on the standard agenda of the right. Though claiming to be "tough on crime," the White House has endorsed a bill that would ease access to handguns for criminals. And conservative sponsors, usually advocates of states' rights, turn a blind eye to the section that overrules state laws against the transportation of firearms.

Selling a gun decontrol bill that hampers law enforcement to senators eager to identify themselves with "law and order" might seem to demand some ingenuity. Senator McClure found a solution that no elected official was likely to oppose: the provisions easing access to guns are balanced by the introduction of mandatory five-year jail terms for all convicted of using a handgun to commit a federal crime. This may make the bill more popular, but it also makes it less just. Mandatory sentences prevent any consideration of extenuating circumstances. If judges are barred from exercising discretion, there will certainly be occasional cases where defendants are sentenced more harshly than they deserve.

Contrary to what the NRA would have us believe, there is no absolute constitutional or moral right to bear arms. The Supreme Court has ruled that the Second Amendment safeguards the collective right of citizens to be protected by an armed militia, not the individual right to carry any type of gun. When 10,000 people are murdered annually with handguns and 500,000 are victims of handgun violence, firearm ownership is not just a private concern of the gun owners and dealers.

The bill may well be right to attack the more onerous restrictions on hunting and sporting rifles. These guns are rarely used by criminals, and under the old law some gun owners have received unduly severe sentences for minor violations. But as for handguns, Congress should strengthen—not relax—the regulations. Sales should be preceded by a compulsory waiting period to allow police time to check whether the purchaser has a criminal record or a history of mental instability. A two-week waiting period would also ward off "impulse" buyers who seek a gun in a moment of passion. (An amendment proposed by Senator Daniel K. Inouye requiring a 14-day waiting period was voted down by 71 to 23.) Firearms owners and dealers should be required by law to report the loss or theft of a handgun. An estimated 60,000 to 200,000 handguns are stolen each year, and many resurface in subsequent crimes. And mandatory gun safety programs should be introduced for all handgun purchasers. Written and practical tests are demanded of drivers. Why not apply the same standards to owners of an even more lethal instrument?

Most handguns have only one purpose—to kill or injure—a function they perform with intolerable efficacy. It requires an element of willful blindness to advocate tough penalties but to scoff at prevention, to piously denounce killing while cherishing the instruments used.

DEFEAT FOR A THIN BLUE LINE[9]

The police were on hand in full force. More than 100 blue-uniformed officers, representing major law-enforcement associations, formed an accusatory gauntlet outside the House of Representatives as Congressmen filed in to consider a bill to loosen federal gun controls. Later, after checking their own side arms, the police filled two sections of the spectators' gallery to watch the debate. Joining them was Sarah Brady, wife of White House Press Secretary James Brady, who was shot and partly paralyzed during John Hinckley's 1981 attack on President Reagan.

Less visible but more formidable was the National Rifle Association, the powerful 3 million–member lobby that had pushed for looser gun controls with a $1.6 million campaign. In the end, N.R.A. muscle spoke louder than the policemen's protests. By a vote of 286 to 136, the House markedly weakened federal regulation of interstate gun trafficking, rewriting restrictions that had been passed in 1968 following the assassinations of Martin Luther King Jr. and Robert Kennedy. The outcome, said Democratic Congressman Robert Torricelli of New Jersey, was "a genuine

[9]Reprint of an article by William R. Doerner, *Time* staffwriter. Reprinted by permission from *Time*, Vol. 127 (Ap. 21, '86), p. 32. Copyright © 1986 by *Time*.

disgrace. It's a classic example of the power of big money and a well-orchestrated campaign by a narrow interest."

The revised law, which is backed by the Administration, would end federal controls on the sale and transport of rifles and shotguns and would simplify record-keeping requirements for gun dealers, allowing them to transfer firearms to "private collections" and sell them unrecorded. Dealers would also be protected from federal prosecution under remaining gun-law restrictions unless authorities can prove that their violations are "willful."

The House tossed a bone to gun-control advocates by continuing the ban on the sale of handguns by dealers in one state to residents of another, a provision strongly endorsed by police organizations. The bill also strengthens penalties for the use of silencers and prohibits the sale of new and used machine guns. The handgun provision means that the bill will have to return to the Senate, which passed a less restrictive version in July, also after vigorous N.R.A. lobbying.

Supporters of liberalizing the 1968 law argue that it was used unfairly against gun dealers who failed to keep adequate records of the sale of firearms and ammunition. The lobby's most effective argument for weakening gun control was still the well-worn Second Amendment guarantee of the right to bear arms. Said Democratic Congressman Harold L. Volkmer of Missouri, sponsor of the House measure: "This body is finally discussing what will truly return constitutional rights to the citizens of this country."

But police officers, who had traditionally been allied with the N.R.A., see weaker gun controls as an increased threat to their lives. Pointing to the police in the galleries, Judiciary Committee Chairman Peter Rodino, a longtime gun foe, declared, "They are here because they recognize that there were 700 or so killed in the last decade [by handguns], and they wonder whether or not they might be next." Only a day after the House action, two FBI agents were killed and five others wounded in Miami as they tried to question two bank robbery suspects who turned on them with an automatic and a shotgun. The casualties were the worst ever suffered by the FBI in a single incident.

III. CONTINUING CONTROVERSY; POLICE CHIEFS VS. THE NRA

EDITOR'S INTRODUCTION

Section Three centers on a new aspect of the continuing controversy over gun control that has arisen during the 1980s, the quarrel that has developed between law-enforcement associations, such as the International Association of Police Chiefs, and the NRA. An article by Bill Lueders, reprinted from the *Progressive*, recounts the disturbing ease with which he obtained handguns from dealers in Milwaukee. George Hackett's article from *Newsweek* focuses on the availability of guns among the very young. Statistics Hackett provides are troubling—that more than 27,000 youths between 12 and 15, for example, were handgun victims in 1985. Youths now bring handguns to school, and in Baltimore sixty percent of high schoolers polled said that they knew of someone who had been shot, threatened, or robbed on school grounds. In Los Angeles youth gangs, financed by the drug trade, protect their turf with submachine guns and assault rifles.

In "Machine Gun U.S.A.," reprinted from *Newsweek*, Tom Morganthau reveals another development in the proliferation of semi-automatic weapons that are designed to kill people in large numbers. These weapons, as Morganthau notes, are wholly unrestricted by federal law, despite the fact that they can easily be converted into automatic weapons capable of firing 1,100 rounds per minute.

In a related article in *U. S. News & World Report*, Ted Gest comments on the NRA's 1987 convention, where a splinter group, the Firearms Coalition, demanded a stronger stand by the NRA in opposing restrictions on machine guns. In conclusion, an article from *Newsweek* reports further on the antagonism between the NRA and law enforcement officers, emphasizing NRA opposition to the banning of plastic guns that can pass undetected through airport security systems. The answer to the problem, says the NRA, is not to ban plastic guns but to improve detection systems.

WRETCHEDNESS IS A WARM GUN[1]

I leaned over the counter, close enough for the salesman to smell the alcohol on my breath. On the left side of my army-green pants was a button that proclaimed, SMASH THE STATE. The button on my jacket was even more to the point: GO REDS/SMASH STATE. With trembling hands I adjusted my Chairman Mao cap.

I was buying a gun—a .25 caliber automatic no bigger than a package of cigarettes. My hands were trembling because I had taken dangerous amounts of legal stimulants. But the man behind the counter didn't know that. And he didn't know whether I was a convicted felon or had just escaped from a mental institution. What's more, the man behind the counter didn't care.

Two years ago, as a reporter for an iconoclastic underground publication called *The Crazy Shepherd*, I went on a gun-buying spree in the Milwaukee area. On the morning of October 25, 1982, I crawled out of bed (with a stinging hangover, after a meager five hours of what passed for sleep) and proceeded to down three Vivarin tablets—a total of 600 milligrams of caffeine alkaloid, the equivalent of at least fifteen cups of coffee—along with three cans of Pabst, all on an empty stomach.

Then I put on my revolutionary outfit, grabbed two more cans of Pabst (to keep the stench of early-in-the-day consumption fresh on my breath), and went looking for a weapon. As identification, I took along the Wisconsin State ID card I had grimaced for years earlier on a post-adolescent lark.

I visited five gun shops in all, picking out the least expensive short-barreled pistol I could find at each, and exiting on the pretense of retrieving my forgotten checkbook after the sale had been written up. Nowhere was I asked *why* I wanted a cheap, easily concealable, inaccurate-except-at-close-range handgun, nor was one ever refused me, despite my intoxicated condition, goofy ID, and aberrant behavior.

[1]Reprint of an article by Bill Lueders. *Progressive* 48:50, N. '84. Reprinted by permission from *The Progressive*, 409 East Main Street, Madison, Wisconsin 53703. Copyright © 1984, The Progressive, Inc.

At Country Outfitters on North 124th Street, I acted jittery and drunk, dropping my car keys twice and expressing dismay when informed of the Wisconsin law requiring a forty-eight-hour "cooling off" period before I could pick up my purchase—a .38 Special revolver nicknamed "The Undercover."

The clerk told me that when I came to claim the gun I would have to fill out a Federal form that asked about such things as whether I was a convicted felon, mentally deranged, or a fugitive from justice. Would the form be given to law-enforcement officials to check if my answers were true? No, came the reply, it would not. "Ever refuse to sell a gun to someone?" I asked. "Only if they answer 'Yes' to one of the questions," he said. What would prevent someone from simply lying on the form? "That's a Federal offense," I was told.

After selecting a .22 caliber snubnose at Dean's Sport and Cycle on Villard Avenue, I inquired uneasily whether a check would be made into my background during the forty-eight-hour waiting period. No, the merchant assured me, there is no such procedure, although it was possible a crosscheck of names might be done at some later date. "The only people who get tripped up," he added, "are people who are on probation or something, but, of course, by then the gun is long gone."

No more Mr. Nice Guy, I resolved over a beer on my way to Spheeris Sporting Goods on North Capital Drive. There, upon locating the cheapest snubnose in stock, I let loose with a depraved laugh. When the salesman got around to me, I pointed to the weapon of my choce and said gruffly, "I want that."

As the clerk wrote up the purchase, I belched beer breath in his face, left monstrous teeth marks in the cap of the pen he lent me, and let saliva dribble out of one corner of my mouth. The clerk was busy and the sale was written up in no time flat. The red star on my cap winked "Thanks" as I left again for my checkbook.

All this happened two years ago, and before retelling the tale here, I had to make sure the results of my peculiar investigation were still valid. And so on August 22, 1984, I went back to Milwaukee on another gun-buying binge.

This time, I wore a Marine Corps camouflage cap. My T-shirt pictured a grinning, beret-capped skull, and emblazoned in stark yellow and red letters was the motto, KILL 'EM ALL/AND LET GOD Sort 'Em Out. I hadn't bathed in a week. I smelled bad and my hair was matted in disgusting clumps. Embarrassed, I slipped on a pair of shades.

I popped eight No-Doz pills (800 milligrams caffeine), washing them down with a six-pack of Pabst—again, on an empty stomach.

Then I went to Flintrop Arms Corporation on West National Avenue and slurred, "I'm been thinking about buying a gun." I chose a .22 caliber pistol that sold for $79.95. The salesman set me up with hollow-point bullets, explaining that they "expand better," as compared to round points, which "just make a clean hole."

The gun, which he said was known as a "belly-buster," was accurate at about twenty feet. The hollow points, which were banned by the Geneva Convention as too insidious for war, had a range of one mile.

Feeling increasingly lousy, I went to Shooters Shop, Inc., on South 84th Street. After choosing a cheap, short-barreled revolver, I was told, to my feigned surprise, about the two-day "cooling off" period. I couldn't wait that long, I said, and opted instead for a used twelve-gauge High Standard shotgun.

As the salesman copied the information from my ID card, I filled out the Federal form. I answered "Yes" to the questions asking whether I was under indictment for a crime, a convicted felon, a fugitive from justice, and an "unlawful user of, or addicted to, marijuana, or a depressant, stimulant, or narcotic drug," only to change my mind to "No." An older clerk saw what I had done and made me fill out another form, this time without the conspicuous crossouts.

My purchase weighed in at just under $150.00, including two boxes of Hunterbrand shells. In a moment, I would be the proud owner of a twelve-gauge shotgun—one of the weapons James Huberty had used to annihilate twenty-one lives at a McDonalds the month before. All I had to do was go outside and retrieve the cash I said was in the glove compartment of my car.

I went outside and threw up.

KIDS: DEADLY FORCE[2]

Two weeks before Christmas Day, 17-year-old Kendall Merriweather was shot and killed a few blocks from his high school in southeast Washington, D.C. Police arrested two teenage students who they believe killed Merriweather while trying to steal his "boom box" radio.

A few days earlier in Pasadena, Texas, a 14-year-old eighth grader at Deepwater Junior High School whipped a snub-nosed .38 out of his jacket and held the assistant principal hostage for two hours. Police said the boy was distraught over his parents' recent separation.

Last week late-evening commuters found the bullet-ridden body of 13-year-old Rolando Mattie at an Oakland, Calif., bus stop. Police believe the seventh-grade dropout was a crack dealer and are looking for five suspects—most of them Mattie's age—in connection with the murder.

These were not isolated incidents. All across America, the number of kids using—and being harmed by—guns is rising at an alarming rate. According to the U.S. Department of Justice, more than 27,000 youths between 12 and 15 were handgun victims in 1985 (the most recent figures), up from an average of 16,500 for each of the three previous years. But officials admit that as grim as those statistics are, they grossly understate the extent of the problem. In recent years, city streets have become flooded with unregistered and untraceable handguns, available to anyone of any age with a bit of cash. In New York, revolvers can be bought on street corners for as little as $25. Some dealers are even willing to "rent" a gun for an evening, deferring payment until the teen can raise money through muggings and robberies. Youth gangs in Los Angeles protect their turf with black-market Uzi submachine guns and Russian-made AK-47 assault rifles, easily financed by the crack trade. Children who live outside urban areas have an even cheaper source of firearms: dad's closet. In California, 38 percent of all households contain a gun. Often, parents don't realize that their .357 magnum or shotgun is missing. "Guns seem to be enjoying a new chic," says handgun expert Garen Wintemute, a Sacramento physician. "The in-

[2]Reprint of an article by George Hackett, *Newsweek* staffwriter. Reprinted by permission from *Newsweek*, vol. III (Ja. 11, '88), pp. 18–19. Copyright © 1988 by *Newsweek*.

creased prevalence of gun carrying among students is reflective of an increased general interest in guns in this country."

Nowhere is the proliferation of firearms among youths more startling than in city high schools. In Baltimore last spring, newly appointed Circuit Judge Ellen Heller was so shocked at the number of minors charged with gun crimes that she ordered a survey of weapon use among students. The results were even worse than she expected. Of 390 city high schoolers polled, 64 percent said they knew someone who had carried a handgun within the preceding six months; 60 percent knew someone who had been shot, threatened or robbed at gunpoint in their school; almost half of the male respondents admitted to having carried a handgun at least once.

Cities with far fewer gun incidents than Baltimore still have plenty to worry about. Twenty years ago, the baddest kid in school carried a switch-blade. But today packing a pistol is a symbol of status and power that others quickly emulate. This snowball effect is reinforced by the climate of fear that a single firearm in the classroom generates. As with adults, many students who say they have no criminal intent start carrying guns to protect themselves from gun-toting class bullies. The child who thinks he's protecting himself, however, is actually putting himself in more danger. Statistics show that kids (and adults) with guns are more likely to be shot than those without guns. "A gun can give someone a sense of power and a security blanket," says Houston psychologist Rion Hart. "They haven't really thought out what they're going to do with it until something happens. But then it's too late." Suddenly, "he said, she said" hallway disputes that were once settled with fists or the flashing of a knife blade end in a burst of fire power and a bloody corpse.

Quick on the trigger: That was how 15-year-old Dartagnan Young died. A freshman at DuSable High School on Chicago's South Side, Young accused a 16-year-old school-mate of slapping his girlfriend. The schoolmate pulled out a .32 revolver and started shooting. As students looked on in horror, Young staggered through the crowded hallway, blood pouring from his chest. He died at the hospital. Often, even less provocation is needed before the bullets begin to fly. "You gotta be prepared—people shoot you for your coat, your rings, chains, anything," says a 15-year-old junior-high-school student in Baltimore, proudly displaying his .25-caliber Beretta.

Much of the increase in gun use stems from urban crack trade. "These [crack] gangs have more firearms than a small police department," says William Newberry, a Bureau of Alcohol, Tobacco and Firearms agent based in Los Angeles. Police say it's typical for street crime to spill over into schools. In ghettos more profound forces may be at work. Children who grow up in broken homes and in the grip of poverty can come to see guns as their only available ticket to prosperity and self-esteem. At the same time, constant exposure to violence on TV and on the street can inure them to the reality of what a bullet can do. "Kids don't care, and they feel life has little value," says Clementine Barfield, whose son Derick was among the 77 youths 16 and under shot dead in Detroit over the past two years. Barfield started SOSAD (Save Our Sons And Daughters) to help other parents overcome their grief and raise awareness of the problem. "We've got to fight for social change, just like we did in the '60s," she says. "We're losing a whole generation of children."

'Make my day': Smaller cities and towns are not immune. Last August a 12-year-old boy in Corpus Christi, Texas, wounded a stockbroker on a crowded downtown street. What most shocked the victim was the way the kid blew the smoke out of his barrel, Clint Eastwood style, then got on his bike and rode away. In De Kalb, Mo., 12-year-old Nathan Faris brought his father's .45 semiautomatic to school one day, seeking revenge on a classmate who had taunted him for being fat. Faris accidently shot a 13-year-old who tried to protect the intended victim, then shot himself in the head. Dr. Deborah Prothrow-Stith, commissioner of the Massachusetts Department of Public Health, attributes outbursts like these to a society too tolerant of violence. "We show that fighting is glamorous on TV—it is rewarded and chosen by the hero as the first solution to a problem," she says. "There's no sorrow, no lamenting when the 'make my day' attitude is put into action."

Whatever the cause, authorities are finding the use of guns by youngsters an extremely difficult trend to stop. Metal detectors, spot searches and increased security have failed to keep guns out of the classroom. Police say it is even harder to keep handguns away from kids on the street. The city of Boston recently launched a TV ad campaign with shocker tag lines such as, "When you tell a friend to fight, you might as well be killing him yourself." But it will take more than commercials to keep schools from becoming modern-day Dodge Cities. As long as pistols are almost as easy to get as candy from a vending machine, people of all ages will continue to end up on both ends of the barrel.

MACHINE GUN U.S.A.[3]

The Rountree brothers lived the fantasy in a squat little building north of Atlanta known as the Bullet Stop. Robert, 32, is an accountant and Bill, 28, is a computer analyst; neither had handled a real machine gun before. But the gun they rented—a Heckler and Koch MP-5—is easy to use and the target was only 10 feet away. Robert cocked the weapon and sighted down the barrel; half a dozen shots boomed out and one of the four bowling pins fell over. Smiling, he flipped the switch to full auto and emptied the H&K's magazine. Two more pins went down, dancing across the concrete as if struck by an invisible whip. "Whee-oo!" yelled Paul Lavista, the Bullet Stop's owner, "Rock and ROLL!" Within 10 minutes, the Rountree brothers had used up 400 rounds of ammunition—enough to hose down any bowling lane. Then they paid Lavista and went home to savor the fun. "It's a rush," said Robert. "It's like a roller coaster or something."

The reality is very different, as Joe Tamarit and Manuel Martinez found out in a San Jose, Calif., motel room one night. Tamarit and Martinez are San Jose cops: in October 1984 they were called to a downtown hostelry on a stolen-credit-card complaint. The innkeeper pointed out a guest named David Wayne Landrum, 26, and Landrum, after a friendly conversation in the lobby, asked Tamarit and Martinez up to his room to discuss the matter in private. They followed him upstairs; Landrum opened the door. Suddenly, he grabbed an UZI assault rifle and opened fire at murderously close range. Tamarit was wounded in the belly and the shoulder. Martinez dove for cover, returning fire with his service revolver: Landrum was wounded. When the siege ended two hours later, police found 150 rounds of ammunition; Landrum had been ready for war. Tamarit spent seven months recuperating, and Martinez still recalls the nightmare moment when he realized they were totally outgunned: within

[3]Reprint of an article by Tom Morganthau, *Newsweek* staffwriter. Reprinted by permission from *Newsweek*, O. 14, '85, pp. 46–51. Copyright © 1985 by *Newsweek*.

seconds Landrum had fired 21 shots to his four. Police Chief Joe McNamara thinks San Jose was lucky—if Landrum had made it to the lobby, the city might have had a massacre on its hands.

Guns don't kill people, criminals do. That homily, a favorite of the National Rifle Association, is true and undeniable. But it is also a fact that America's long love affair with the gun has entered a new and dangerous phase—a nationwide craze for the most exotic, most powerful and most lethal small arms on the wide-open U.S. market. Hunting rifles are passé, except for hunters, and handguns are commonplace; by some estimates, Americans now own 65 million pistols and revolvers, two handguns for every three households. And so, for perhaps the last five years, the hot sellers in many gunshops have been modern combat weapons. Perhaps 500,000 military-style assault guns are now in private hands in the United States. They are small and light and easy to handle, the cream of small-arms technology and the mainstay of commandos and security forces the world over. The UZI, made famous by the Israeli Army and used by the U.S. Secret Service, is one such gun. The MAC-10, designed during the Vietnam era, is another. The AR-15, which is the civilian version of the Army's M-16, is another, and there are many, many more— H&K's, Steyrs and KG-99s, all sophisticated paramilitary weapons that were designed with only one purpose in mind, to kill human beings in large numbers very quickly.

The fascination with rapid-fire weapons has many origins— some deeply rooted in the American experience, some as ephemeral as fad. Take a gun collector like Donald Hitzhusen of Rockwell, Iowa, and he will tell you that he has *always* had guns—grew up with guns, likes guns, collects exotic military guns, of which he has many. A hobby. Others, like Robert and Bill Rountree, got the urge to grease a few bowling pins after watching an Arnold Schwarzenegger movie on cable TV—"The Terminator," which is only one of a growing number of films and TV shows featuring the latest in high-tech, maxi-violence weaponry. Some say the Secret Service started it all in 1981: TV coverage of Ronald Reagan's close encounter with John Hinckley showed a presidential bodyguard pulling a UZI from under his jacket. Others point to Vietnam, the first war in which most infantrymen routinely used automatic weapons like the M-16 in combat. And finally, there is the widespread fascination with paramilitary survival training—the sense, as melodramatically depicted in movies like "Invasion U.S.A.," that the average citizen, if trained and heavily armed, can somehow defend his own when Armageddon comes.

In fact, the exotic-weapons craze is nowhere more frightening than among fanatics of the far right—a loosely knit underground of racist, anti-Semitic, pseudo-Christian xenophobes with links to both the Ku Klux Klan and the American Nazi movement. Ten members of one such group, The Order, are currently on trial in Seattle for a variety of serious crimes that include the murder of Alan Berg, the Denver radio-talk-show host who was assassinated on June 18, 1984. The alleged hit man was arrested in Georgia with a van crammed full of military weapons and explosives. The gun allegedly used in Berg's murder was a .45-caliber MAC-10, and it was allegedly supplied by a member of a group called the Covenant, the Sword and the Arm of the Lord. CSA has a camp on the Arkansas-Missouri border that until recently boasted both a paramilitary training area and a well-equipped gunshop: in a raid on the camp last April, federal and state investigators seized an arsenal that included 77 semiautomatic rifles and machine guns. Berg, according to government witnesses, was gunned down outside his home with a one-second, 13-shot burst from the MAC-10—and the gun, fitted with a silencer, made about as much noise as an electric drill.

Even common criminals are acquiring uncommon arms. If law-abiding Americans now have a yen for exotic weapons, some law-enforcement officials say the underworld is involved in something like an arms race. The MAC-10 has become the side arm of choice for "cocaine cowboys" and other drug smugglers: south Florida, that bastion of drug smuggling on the East Coast, is said to be jampacked with MAC's and other military guns. "South Florida is the mecca of illegal automatics, and machine-gun hits are almost commonplace," says Edward D. Conroy, who heads the Miami office of the U.S. Bureau of Alcohol, Tobacco and Firearms. "There are even brazen attacks at stoplights, with grandma and the kiddies getting greased along with the target." UZI's, MAC's and other automatics are showing up in bank heists and holdups elsewhere in the nation as well: three jewelry-store bandits recently sprayed the lobby of Los Angeles's Beverly Wilshire Hotel with an UZI, for example, and police in suburban San Francisco are puzzling over a chain of robberies by someone equipped with a gun that also looks like an UZI. The puzzle, in this instance, is why the stickup man would bother—his robberies have all been nickel-dime affairs at fast-food outlets.

It was a lazy Sunday afternoon in August and some 2,000 people from the West Indies Cricket Club were picnicking at a 50-acre recreation complex in Oakland, N.J. Suddenly, chaos: a shot, two shots, a burst of gunfire, then bullets flying in all directions in what seemed, for about 10 minutes, to be a scene from downtown Beirut. When it was over, authorities seized 37 semiautomatic guns and a MAC-11. Two men were dead and 19 persons were wounded, including a woman and a boy. Although investigators speculate that the mayhem was triggered by a dispute over drugs, no one is really sure why the fire fight began. "We're not used to this blatant display of gunfire," says Bergen County prosecutor Dennis Calo. "What happened defies description."

There are no reliable statistics on the number of such guns in private hands in the United States today, because the federal government does not require registration or licensing of any weapon so long as it is not, technically, a machine gun. A machine gun is a weapon that fires repeating shots with one pull of the trigger; the seller must record the serial number and the buyer must be fingerprinted and pass a background check. *Semiautomatic* weapons, which require a separate trigger pull for each shot, are wholly unrestricted by federal law, no matter how closely they approximate the firepower of a machine gun. Many popular sport weapons are capable of semiautomatic fire—and so are most paramilitary "grease guns." The MAC-10, for example, is marketed legally (and cheaply) in its semiautomatic version, known as the SM-10. A MAC-10 on full auto empties a 30-shot magazine in three seconds; the SM-10 can do the same thing in five seconds. To anyone on the receiving end, as San Jose police investigator Moses Reyes observes, "it really doesn't make much difference."

Further—and this is crucial—a thriving gray market has sprung up for so-called "conversion kits" that enable gun owners to turn a legal semiautomatic, like an AR-15, into a restricted full automatic—an M-16. The MAC-10 is so easy to convert that ATF ultimately reclassified it as a machine gun, which sharply reduced its sales. The AR-15 is easy too: even a novice can convert the gun to full automatic with a mail-order kit of seven parts and one special piece of contraband called a "drop-in auto sear," a Z-

shaped piece of metal about two inches long whose sale is, theo-
retically at least, restricted by federal law. Mail-order conversion
kits for many guns were widely advertised in gun magazines until
relatively recently, and they are still available from dealers. No
one knows how many were sold, or for which guns, and no one
knows how many semiautomatic weapons have actually been converted to full automatic by private owners. Technically, all con-
versions require a machine-gun license—but in practice, the law
is largely unenforceable.

The Bureau of Alcohol, Tobacco and Firearms polices the
market for automatic weapons and conversion kits, mostly by going after dealers and manufacturers who neglect its requirements
for record keeping on sales and serial numbers. As a result, ATF
is the only federal agency that collects statistics on the sale of military weapons in the United States—but its statistics, which are
predicated on the increasingly tenuous distinction between machine guns and other military guns, are suggestive at best. Over
the last three years, the ATF reports, its seizures of illegal machine guns have more than tripled, from 871 guns and conversion kits in 1983 to 3,263 in 1985. (The number does not include
weapons seized by other agencies, such as the FBI, the Drug Enforcement Administration or state and local police.) Over the last
five years the number of persons licensed to sell machine guns
also has tripled, and the number of machine guns being sold legally—ATF provides no actual numbers for this—has risen by
about 60 percent. American dealers are importing an average of
55,000 foreign-made machine guns each year; to judge by the
number of inquiries from foreign governments for ATF's investi-
gative assistance, the number of machine guns sold by Americans
to overseas buyers is also rising sharply. "We're kind of the 'Guns-
R-Us' for a large part of the world," an ATF agent jokes.

Calculating the number of assault weapons in American
homes is a complicated matter. The estimate of 500,000 comes
from a gun-control lobbyist, Michael Hancock, who is general
counsel for the National Coalition to Ban Handguns. Hancock
guesses that perhaps 125,000 of those guns have been converted
to full automatic. Sales figures collected by ATF indicate that
more than 300,000 AR-15s have been sold as semiautomatics
since the gun was approved for the civilian market. In addition,
some 36,000 MAC-10s were sold between 1979 and 1982, when
ATF at last restricted its sale. Add to those statistics about 5,000

KG-9s and a genuinely incalculable number of UZI's, H&K's and other guns, and Hancock's cautiously ventured estimate is that about half a million such weapons are now in private hands. ATF's chief weapons expert, Frank W. (Bill) Nickell, concurs: "I would accept that," Nickell says. (The 500,000 total does not include the number of *licensed* machine guns in private hands, which also is rising: currently, ATF records show 116,000 licensed automatic weapons of all types nationwide.)

The numbers underscore the fact that military guns have acquired a powerful allure for millions of Americans—and it is by no means true that all those who covet UZI's or AR-15s or H&K MP-5s have some secret wish to use them on other human beings. The Bullet Stop's owner, Paul Lavista, says his clientele includes a "big cadre" of solid citizens—lawyers, salesmen, airline pilots—who are simply intrigued by the novelty and glamour of automatic weapons; and he says that none of his customers are "closet crazies." Other aficionados, such as Robert K. Brown, publisher of *Soldier of Fortune* magazine, stoutly defend their right to own and use such guns for sport or self-defense despite the disapproval of the gun-control lobby. The liberals have inflamed the public's fears about guns, the argument goes, and the media often ignores the fact that the vast majority of American gun owners are law-abiding, responsible citizens. And it is probably true, as Tulane University sociologist Joe Sheley says, that the fad for combat weapons poses little direct threat to the public at large. "It looks like a lot of them are going to a few people," he says. "The extent to which any of us is going to cross paths with one of these people is small."

Cops who have seen the business end of a loaded grease gun, however, take an understandably darker view. They say the spread of military guns means trouble, possibly big trouble, when the guns get in the wrong hands, and they tend to regard the owners of such weapons as either criminals or dangerous kooks. "The last UZI we seized was taken from a woman who thought she was under attack by laser beams from Mars," says San Jose's Joe McNamara. "It's a ridiculous situation: there aren't many controls on handguns, and there aren't *any* controls on [semiautomatic rifles]. The cops can't protect you—they can't even protect themselves."

A case in point, from the files of the Oakland, Calif., police department, was a bizarre incident last April involving a troubled 34-year-old man named Dennis Cresta. Cresta appeared on Telegraph Avenue one Sunday afternoon wearing camouflage fatigues and carrying two semiautomatic rifles, a Ruger Mini 14 and an AR-15. Questioned by a California highway patrolman, police say, he opened fire without warning and riddled the patrolman's cruiser with high-velocity rounds. The officer, pinned down in the front seat, radioed for help and police cordoned off the street. Cresta emptied one gun and kept on firing with the other, spraying the neighborhood with bullets for nearly an hour. Miraculously, though a police officer and a bystander in a nearby restaurant were cut by flying glass, no one was actually shot. Cresta finally surrendered and was charged with six counts of attempted murder. He told police he was frustrated by difficulties he encountered in going to Alaska.

The obvious question is whether government is doing enough to protect the public from the inevitable risks of this widespread escalation in civilian firepower. The answer is probably no—but given the politics of gun control, there is little likelihood that the federal government will take a more aggressive stance. Stephen Higgins, director of ATF, is concerned by the spread of illegally converted assault guns, but the bureau's position on enforcement policy is that no new laws are needed. Currently, ATF officials have high hopes for a pending prosecution against the principals in S.W.D., Inc., of Atlanta for allegedly conspiring to sell unregistered MAC-10s. (The firm's president, Sylvia W. Daniels, denies wrongdoing.) ATF also won a key legal battle in 1982 when a federal judge upheld its decision to regulate the sale of MAC-10s and KG-9s as machine guns. Meanwhile, bureau agents pursue dealers and criminals who trade in illegal automatic guns and conversion kits. In south Florida, two young ATF agents have been murdered since 1982, which may be a gruesome measure of their success at infiltrating the drugs-and-guns underworld. Last June, moreover, ATF scored a publicity coup of sorts by arresting a south Florida auto dealer for offering to sell automatic weapons. It was a case of life imitating art—the suspect, who has pleaded innocent on the charges, was driving the Corvette-powered Ferrari that is featured on "Miami Vice."

For the most part, however, ATF is pursuing a narrow, legalistic and highly technical enforcement strategy that sidesteps the crux of the problem—the wholly legal sale of paramilitary guns in their semiautomatic versions. The basic legal distinction—automatics bad, semiautomatics good—dates back to 1934, when honest Americans had deer rifles and only gangsters had Tommy guns. Given the killing capabilities of modern military weaponry, however, the distinction has less and less relevance to real-world law enforcement: converted or not, an UZI is a fearsome piece of hardware. In California, state Assemblyman Art Agnos filed a bill to restrict the sale of military-style semiautomatic weapons just as machine-gun sales are restricted; the bill went nowhere in the Assembly's last session and Agnos withdrew it. Though California already restricts the sale of automatic weapons more than most states, police and ATF agents say its gun laws have largely failed to slow the spread of mail-order military guns from out-of-state dealers.

The outlook is no brighter in Washington, where a handful of congressional gun-control advocates are struggling to reform federal law. One bill, sponsored by House Judiciary Committee chairman Peter Rodino and Rep. William Hughes, both New Jersey Democrats, would simply ban the sale of machine guns and silencers to civilian owners—though currently licensed machine guns could remain in private hands. Rep. Robert Torricelli, another New Jersey Democrat, has proposed a bill to expand ATF's ban on the MAC-10, making the 36,000 MAC-10s sold between 1979 and 1982 retroactively illegal. The political momentum in Congress, however, seems to be going the other way: in July the Senate passed a bill sponsored by Sen. James McClure of Idaho and Rep. Harold Volkmer of Missouri to make machine-gun ownership *easier*—and liberals are even nervous about the chances for passing another Hughes bill to ban Teflon-coated "cop killer" bullets.

Torricelli, for one, says the United States is "facing gun control as if this were the last century," and he cites the much-feared political clout of the gun lobby for stifling even the most rudimentary reform legislation in Congress. He contends that "no reasonable public policy can include the right of the citizen to possess machine guns," which seems a plausible argument to most liberals. But there is little evidence that his colleagues and the voters are listening.

DISSIDENTS, OLD ALLIES SHAKE NRA[4]

Going into its annual convention this weekend in Reno, Nev., the National Rifle Association seems at odds with itself, one of the more unlikely victims of institutional schizophrenia. The same body that strode for years like a gladiator across the political playing field, obliterating virtually every gun-control proposal from the U.S. Capitol to local town halls, has lately become the victim of its own success, facing fire from its own members for losing major battles on legislation banning the manufacture of machine guns and armor-piercing bullets.

"For the first time," says John Nichols of the Oregon State Rifle and Pistol Association, citing the constitutional right to keep and bear arms, "the Second Amendment didn't mean what it says."

Predictably, leaders of the NRA reject accusations that the organization has compromised members' rights. But even as the NRA moves to stem the rising tide of criticism, it is becoming increasingly evident that the once feared gun lobby is wrestling with a perplexing identity crisis. "Their idea of negotiation," says the NRA's former chief lobbyist, Neal Knox, "is deciding whether you should have your arm taken off at the shoulder or at the wrist." At issue are not just the political fortunes of the NRA but—in a very real sense—the shape of firearms legislation in the United States for several years to come.

Knox, who would like NRA members to install him as chief executive at the Reno convention, now leads the Firearms Coalition—a group of NRA members who want the organization to take a harder line against the "anti-gunners." His appeal strikes a chord in many quarters. Arizona state Senator Wayne Stump, calling NRA leaders too devoted to the "Washington cocktail circuit," says that "in the politics of give and take, they think it's always give."

[4]Reprint of an article by Ted Gest, *U.S. News & World Report* staffwriter. Reprinted by permission from *U.S. News & World Report*, Ap. 27, '87, p. 44. Copyright © 1987 by *U.S. News & World Report*.

Machine-Gunners Upset

NRA stalwarts aren't the only ones taking potshots at the group. Machine-gun enthusiasts—angry that Congress halted production of their favorite weapon—have formed their own group, the National Firearms Association, to seek a reversal on Capitol Hill. An officer, Paige Massey of Austin, Tex., says the NRA fell down on its historic role to defend all firearms. "It should have adopted a NATO doctrine," says Massey, "that an attack on one gun-owner group is an attack on all."

As if dissent within the ranks were not enough, the NRA also has managed to offend one of its staunchest allies—the police. Complaining that police officers are being faced more and more often with automatic-weapons fire and ammunition that can penetrate "bulletproof" vests, law-enforcement authorities broke ranks with the NRA over the 1986 gun bill. At its annual meeting last year, the International Association of Chiefs of Police took the unprecedented step of banning the NRA from setting up a booth. Jerald Vaughn, director of the chiefs' association, calls the NRA "one of the most potentially dangerous organizations in the United States today."

On yet another front, the NRA finds itself plagued by strife within it own headquarters in Washington, D.C. In the midst of the congressional gun-control fight last year, the NRA dismissed its chief executive, G. Ray Arnett, in a messy internal dispute that reportedly cost the group $400,000—to avoid a lawsuit. At the same time, NRA membership was declining from a high of 3 million a few years ago to an estimated 2.7 million today.

Election Maneuvering

In the center of the storm is J. Warren Cassidy, who succeeded Knox as NRA lobbyist and then took over the top job after Arnett's firing. Critics accuse Cassidy of being too quick to surrender to Capitol Hill opponents, even though NRA's outpouring of $1.6 million to congressional campaigns should easily have given it the upper hand. Cassidy, who contends he has been treated unfairly in the press, refused to give interviews before the Reno meeting. He did appear recently in a rare debate against Knox before gun buffs in Portland, Oreg. Cassidy angered some by saying that the NRA would not seek to overturn the machine-gun ban in Congress but might contest it in court on constitutional grounds.

If there is a shooting match at this weekend's convention, Cassidy may have a crucial andvantage. NRA leaders had members vote by mail before the meeting to allow the group's 75-member board to select the new chief executive—a decision Knox will challenge in Reno as a turnabout from the membership revolt in 1977, which launched the NRA on the road to being a powerful lobbying force.

Organizations that lobby for gun control are taking scant comfort from the NRA's woes. Says Barbara Lautman of Handgun Control, Inc., which seeks restraints such as records checks for prospective gun owners: "We're talking about a fight between extremists and ultra-extremists."

Whatever happens in Reno, the NRA is not about to fade away. It has been successful, for instance, in persuading 28 states to prohibit localities from passing gun-control laws, and it is working for passage of similar laws elsewhere. The big question now for the NRA is whether it can settle its problems and regain it preeminent position. "The only power that can stop NRA," says John Aquilino, the group's former communications director, "is the NRA itself."

BATTLE OVER THE PLASTIC GUN[5]

NRA Shoot-out on Capitol Hill

Cop-killer bullets, mail-order handguns, machine guns . . . Has the NRA gone off the deep end?"

The man attacking the National Rifle Association's guns-at-any-cost zeal in the full-page ad that ran in major newspapers two weeks ago is not the type one usually associates with gun-control groups. In fact, he's a man who carries a gun himself: Joseph McNamara, the chief of police of San Jose, Calif. A few years ago it

[5]Reprint of an article by George Hackett, *Newsweek* staffwriter. Reprinted by permission from *Newsweek*, vol. 109 (Je. 1, '87), p. 31. Copyright © 1989 by *Newsweek*.

would have been unthinkable for a policeman like McNamara to speak out against the 3 million–member NRA. "I used to think they were on my side," says McNamara. But recent NRA campaigns—notably its push to legalize Teflon-coated ammunition that can penetrate bulletproof vests—has turned many law-enforcement groups against the gun lobby.

The NRA last year lost the fight over the armor-piercing slugs, as well as its effort to permit private ownership of machine guns. But the group is at it again, this time lobbying against legislation to restrict plastic guns that can pass undetected through airport security systems. "These weapons are for war and combat and have no place in urban society," says McNamara, referring to the so-called terrorist specials. "But the NRA leaders seem to have lost any sense of responsibility."

Terrorist tool: Plastic guns first received wide attention a year ago when Libyan President Muammar Kaddafi tried to buy 100 Austrian-made Glock 17 pistols, which are part plastic and part metal. In Washington, Rep. Mario Biaggi of New York demonstrated why terrorists favor the plastic gun by having an aide smuggle a dismantled Glock 17 past the Capitol's metal detector. But legislators are even more concerned with what the Glock 17 forebodes: a new generation of completely nonmetal guns that would be even easier to conceal. At congressional hearings last week, gun manufacturer David Byron testified that his Florida company will have a prototype for an all-plastic gun within nine to 15 months.

Congress wants to set "a standard of detectability" that would ban firearms that fail to trigger metal detectors and X-ray machines currently in use (the legislation would not apply to military or police sales). But even that restriction is too much for the NRA. "Why focus on something that is a year away?" asks NRA lobbyist James Jay Baker, who advocates improving detection systems rather than banning plastic guns. NRA spokesman David Warner has a more general argument: he says the lobby opposes any legislation that "seeks to ban a particular type of firearm."

That kind of tunnel vision could damage the NRA more than any gun-control group has managed to do. Both the International Association of Police Chiefs and the rank-and-file Fraternal Order of Police favor the ban on plastic firearms as well as legislation—opposed by the NRA—to institute a seven-day waiting period for all handgun sales. Police officers are not the only ones turning away from the NRA: membership in the organization has dropped 200,000 since last year. The NRA blames the decline on a $5 increase in annual dues, but McNamara, who is used to getting hate mail from gun advocates, has lately been receiving letters from NRA members who agree with his position. "Some people think it's strange," says McNamara, "to be supporting plastic guns for terrorists." This time the gun lobby just may have shot itself in the foot.

IV. RECENT COURT AND STATE INITIATIVES

EDITOR'S INTRODUCTION

This section reviews action on gun control in the courts and in state legislatures. In the opening article, "Guns in the Courts," reprinted from the *Atlantic*, Elaine F. Weiss explains that anti-gun forces have initiated an effort to restrict the flow of guns through the courts by bringing lawsuits for product liability against gun manufacturers. Although the initiative may very well not succeed, its sponsors hope that it will bring pressure to bear on gun makers through increased insurance costs, so that it will no longer be feasible for them to make Saturday night specials.

Several other articles comment on developments at the state level. An article in *The Economist* reports on the enactment of a new gun law in the state of Florida making handguns more widely available. Mary McIver, writing in *Maclean's*, also comments on the new Florida law, pointing out that the murder rate in Miami is now the highest in the country and that the Floridians' answer to more guns in the hands of criminals is more guns available to citizens. In a following article from *U. S. News & World Report*, it is noted that the state of Maryland has recently followed an entirely different course from that of Florida, voting to ban the cheap handguns often used in street crimes and family squabbles. At present no consistent pattern in the control of handguns exists among the states. It is still possible to obtain a Saturday night special that is banned in one state by crossing over the border into the next. This lack of consistency in the regulation of guns seems part of a larger failure of public consensus on the issue.

GUNS IN THE COURTS[1]

The bitter debate over gun control, which for two decades has taken place in Congress, state houses, and city halls, is being carried into the courtroom. With this change in venue comes a change in the shape of the issue. A new strategy is emerging, one that purposefully circumvents the legislative process, tries to avoid the usual constitutional argument about the right to bear arms, and instead calls forth the citizen's right of legal redress.

Almost sixty lawsuits are now pending in which victims of handgun shootings are suing the manufacturers and distributors of the cheap, concealable guns with short barrels called "snubbies" or Saturday Night Specials. Phillip Corboy is the lawyer representing the widow and family of James Riodan, the highest-ranking police officer ever killed in the line of duty in Chicago, in their suit against Walther, the West German manufacturer, and International Armament Corporation, the American distributor of the gun used to kill Riordan. In Washington, D.C., Jacob Stein, a lawyer acting on behalf of presidential press secretary James Brady and his wife, Sarah, drew up a suit against another German gun manufacturer, Roehm GmgH., and its American importing facility, RG Industries, Inc., demanding $100 million for damages inflicted by their product—John Hinckley's gun. Windle Turley, a Dallas lawyer, has filed nineteen similar lawsuits in nine states.

All these cases are based upon an unconventional and as yet unproven application of product-liability law, the law made famous by the suits against the Corvair and Pinto automobiles. The lawyers and their clients do not contend that the making or selling of handguns is illegal, or that the manufacturers are guilty of a crime. Neither do they seek a court-ordered ban on these guns. What they do contend is that these handguns, which took 22,000 lives in America last year, are built and sold with no purpose other than to kill people, and that the harm they inflict upon society is so great that the manufacturers who profit from them should be held financially responsible for the damage they cause. The

[1]Reprint of an article by Elaine F. Weiss, free-lance writer. Reprinted by permission from *Atlantic*, Vol. 251 (My. '83), pp. 8–16. Copyright © 1983 by *Atlantic*.

plaintiffs and their counselors are trying to stimulate an economic incentive for gun control: if manufacturers are held liable for damages, they will either pay exorbitant rates for their insurance or lose it altogether, leaving them little choice but to keep a tighter rein on gun sales or get out of the business.

The idea of using product liability against handgun manufacturers was first brought before the public by Stuart Speiser, a New York tort attorney, in his book *Lawsuit*, published in 1980. In a chapter entitled "The Ultimate Deterrent: Taking on the Gun Lobby," Speiser called on "inventive" tort lawyers to carry product liability "one step further and bring the great power of our civil courts to bear on a problem that our legislatures and criminal courts have not been able to solve." Presenting an array of product-liability precedents and dram-shop common law (holding suppliers of liquor responsible for injuries that result from serving liquor to an intoxicated person), Speiser outlined ways to support lawsuits that could hurt gun suppliers financially.

The concept also occurred to Turley in 1980, and he began investigating its potential. Turley, a litigation lawyer known for his creative use of tort law, assigned the building of a liability case against gunmakers to his firm's research-and-development department, allotting it a budget of several hundred thousand dollars and two full-time attorneys. Long an ardent supporter of gun control, Turley has become something of a crusader, giving public lectures on the new legal strategy of using product-liability law, conducting law-school symposia, writing law-review articles, and even submitting to the questioning of Mike Wallace, on *60 Minutes*. More important, he has encouraged fellow lawyers to try the strategy in court—for example, traveling to Washington to urge Jacob Stein to use it in the Brady case. About sixty cases had been filed by the end of last year; Turley's "conservative estimate" is that more than 200 suits will be on the dockets by the end of this year.

A citizen's-advocacy organization based in Washington, Handgun Control, Inc., plans to become a national information clearinghouse, where victims of handgun violence can learn of the legal actions available to them and obtain a list of lawyers willing to take on their cases; lawyers will be able to find a repository of books and legal briefs for preparing suits.

While Stuart Speiser still waits for a case strong enough to test his original ideas, and Jacob Stein tries to keep a low profile in a case whose participants cannot avoid worldwide attention, Windle Turley is courting the press, and has emerged as the dominant legal practitioner in the new field. Even though his opponents honor him by labeling the legal initiatives against suppliers "the Turley angle" or "the Turley routine" or "the Turley fixation," the true paternity of the strategy doesn't matter. As Mark Wooster, an editor of the *Harvard Law Review* who is analyzing these cases, points out, all the lawyers involved will be trying to prove that the legal ideas they are presenting are *not* their own. "Originality is a sin in law," he says. "All you want is precedent."

Critics of these cases—and there are many—consider them to be totally without legal precedent, and without merit. They see them as a sinister manipulation of the court system by zealous reformers bent on achieving their political goals, or as the actions of a bunch of greedy lawyers looking for new sources of income, or as a plot to shift the culpability of the criminal onto businessmen.

The cases have attracted an unusual amount of attention. *The New York Times* applauded the suit brought by James Brady in an editorial published last summer. The staff of Senator Edward Kennedy, which pours its energies into the Senate's doomed gun-control bills, offered the legal efforts its blessing. The attitude of President Reagan toward the suit his friend Brady is bringing can only be surmised, but a close confidant of the president, Senator Paul Laxalt, wrote a fierce indictment of the strategy in his preface to a monograph called "Turning the Gun on Tort Law: Aiming at Courts to Take Products Liability to the Limit," published by the Washington Legal Foundation, a conservative legal think-tank. One of the attorneys for the defense in Brady's case is Paul D. Kamenar, a staff lawyer for the Washington Legal Foundation.

The lawyers pleading for the plaintiffs see their legal strategy as a logical extension and amplification of concepts already firmly established in tort law. A brief explanation of legal definitions will help make clear the foundation of these lawsuits.

Tort law is a system of justice meant to deter unreasonable behavior, and, failing that, to allow compensation for injury caused by dangerous behavior. Torts usually concern the harm inflicted by one person on another, even if no criminal actions take place, and are usually remedied by the paying of damages, as in auto-accident cases. Product liability is a subdivision of tort law that holds the makers and sellers of products responsible for any harm the products cause consumers. Manufacturers can be found liable if they fail to meet certain "duties of care" to the public. The three standards of care being applied in these cases are: *Negligence*—the manufacturer could foresee the harm his product might cause but failed to take "reasonable care" to prevent it. *Strict liability*—makers and sellers of products that prove to have a "defect" that makes them "unreasonably dangerous" must bear special responsibilities. *Absolute liability*—those who pursue "abnormally dangerous" or "ultrahazardous" activities are liable for any harm that might be caused by their actions or products.

The dividing lines between these standards for judging liability are blurry, and the categories often overlap. Each of the lawsuits already filed employs a combination of all three, depending on the factual circumstances of the particular case and the statutory and common law of the state where it will be decided. When the cases come to trial, the attorneys will have to prove to the judges that their clients have a legitimate claim under the doctrines of product liability. They will concentrate especially on establishing their claims of strict liability, which, as a species of no-fault liability, impugns not the actions of the manufacturer but only the defective product. Strict liability is easier than absolute liability to prove as a matter of law, and easier than negligence to prove as a matter of fact.

In order for a court to hold a manufacturer strictly liable, the plaintiff must show that the product contained a defect; that this defect caused the product to be unreasonably dangerous; and that it inflicted harm. A precise definition of "defect" has not yet been articulated by the courts, and is the subject of continuing legal dispute. Nonetheless, three general categories of defect have been established—those arising in a product's design, in its manufacture, or in its marketing.

The emphasis in the cases coming to trial will be on the alleged "design defect" of handguns, though some suits also claim a "marketing defect."

The gist of the plaintiffs' arguments for holding gun manufacturers and sellers strictly liable is the following sequence of assertions: Small-caliber (less than .38), short-barreled (3-inch or less), lightweight, inexpensive ($50 or less), easily concealable handguns are designed, manufactured, and distributed principally for shooting people; this kind of gun is not sufficiently accurate or reliable for sporting use, military or police functions, or even for self-defense; these properties make the gun "defective" by design; these handguns, having no purpose other than to injure and kill, are of no benefit to society; they are indiscriminately marketed to the general public without proper precautions or screening of buyers; this type of marketing is "defective"; the design defect of handguns, when coupled with the marketing defect, creates an unreasonably dangerous situation and risk of harm to society.

The plaintiffs are using the term "defect" in its broadest possible meaning, almost in the sense of a social defect, and the defendants insist that this definition is so broad as to be meaningless. They insist that the plaintiffs must show that the particular gun used in each instance was mechanically defective—that something was specifically wrong, such as a faulty trigger, that made it unsafe. A handgun is not defective simply because it can shoot bullets, the defendants say; that is its natural function and the reason it is purchased.

There are two tests that can be used by the court to determine if a design is defective. The traditional one, the "consumer-expectation test," recognizes a defective product as one that fails to meet the reasonable expectations of the ordinary consumer that it will be safe in normal and intended use. The second one, which has emerged only in the past few years but is quickly gaining acceptance, is the "risk/utility balancing test," in which the risk of injury posed by the design of the product is weighed against the benefit of the product to society. The defendants lean heavily on the consumer-expectation test, because it is true that guns are bought with the thought of eventually shooting someone, and they meet that expectation. The plaintiffs will try to persuade the courts to employ the risk/utility test.

"Injury or death is not a socially acceptable benefit of a product," Windle Turley writes in the complaint of Diane Moore v. Roehm GmbH. Balancing the risk that handguns are known to pose to American society (an average of fifty deaths a day, hundreds of thousands of injuries a year, and millions of dollars in medical expenses) against their utility as a destructive tool must tip the scales in favor of the public safety, he contends.

But handguns do have social utility, the defendants reply: they are used by hunters of small game and undercover law-enforcement officers, and, especially, by law-abiding citizens, for self-protection. The plaintiffs refute these claims with statistics on the number of states that ban hunting with small-caliber weapons and the overwhelming preference of hunters for long guns. They cite the distinct differences between the large, finely crafted handguns used in police work and the cheap street guns under discussion, and offer some startling numbers on the ineffectiveness of handguns as an implement for self-defense: studies have found that the assault victim who offers armed resistance is anywhere from two to eight times more likely to be hurt or killed in the attempt than one who offers no resistance.

It was not a handgun that shot the plaintiffs or their kin, the defendants say, or even a jealous lover or a nervous homeowner. It was a *criminal* who shot them—a variation on the standard "Guns don't kill people, people kill people" refrain. Even if the gun could be proven "defective," the defect did not cause the harm, an intervening, unforeseen criminal did—and this breaks the legal chain of causation and sets the manufacturer free from liability. To this the plaintiffs respond that in stict liability, as opposed to negligence, the actions of neither the producer nor the user are in question, only the product itself, and the intervention of a criminal does not preclude a claim. They also say that the usual focus on criminal use of handguns is misplaced and misleading, because handguns are equally lethal in the hands of the general public. According to FBI crime analyses, fewer than 15 percent of handgun homicides were actually premeditated murders—most were impulsive shootings of family, friends or neighbors during quarrels, or accidental shootings, or suicides (a full 50 percent of all handgun deaths are suicides).

The plaintiffs argue that it is the compounding of the handguns' defective design with a defective distribution chain that creates the unreasonably dangerous situation deserving of strict liability. Distribution also enters into the plaintiffs' claims of negligence, which are, in essence: that manufacturers made a conscious business decision to design this kind of handgun so as to make it concealable, sell it cheaply, and market it indiscriminately; that because of these properties, handguns are the "weapon of choice" among criminals (50 percent of murders, 40 percent of robberies, and 23 percent of aggravated assaults are committed with them); that the defendants knew or could foresee that their handguns would be used in crime; that they did not take proper precautions to keep their guns out of the possession of people "psychologically unfit" to have them; that the manufacturers and distributors were thus negligent in their responsibility to the public.

The plaintiffs' briefs suggest that a stringent police check of all prospective gun buyers be routine, and that a mandatory waiting period be imposed in order to curtail impulse purchases (the Kennedy/Rodino bill, pending in Congress, would have all states implement these). The defendants point out existing state and local ordinances requiring gun buyers to fill out forms revealing any police record and attesting to their mental stability, and statutes requiring police checks and possession permits. The manufacturers and distributors insist that they are in compliance with all current rules and cannot be made liable when they have obeyed the law. But many gun dealers do not enforce the rules that do exist, the plaintiffs say, and the manufacturers and distributors have an obligation to oversee the dealers and, if necessary, withdraw their guns from shops known to give guns to anyone who will plunk down his money. Should all these measures prove unworkable, the plaintiffs' briefs continue, the manufacturers should restrict the sale of their handguns to the military, the police, and authorized sporting clubs.

Foreseeability is a key element in proving negligence. The defense asserts that manufacturers do not intend and cannot foresee that their guns might fall into the hands of people who will use them in criminal acts. They are meant for good citizens who will use them only for sport or self-protection, and suppliers cannot be held accountable for their products' being intentionally misused. In rebuttal, the plaintiffs quote more statistics. Manufacturers may intend their handguns for the solid citizen, they say, but in truth handguns are the number-one weapon of crime: while they represent fewer than 20 percent of the privately owned firearms in the nation, they account for 90 percent of gun-related deaths and injuries. An estimated 100,000 handguns are stolen out of the homes of those solid citizens every year and used in crime. New handguns are far more likely to be used in crime than old ones, and 2.4 million new ones are introduced into this country every year.

Absolute liability is a rare and difficult standard to impose, and is usually applied only to those engaged in the "ultra-hazardous" production of certain drugs, explosives, toxic chemicals, and nuclear devices. But in their lawsuits, Stein and

Corboy ask the court to find the gunmakers absolutely liable for introducing "abnormally dangerous instrumentalities of no social value and contrary to public policy . . . into the channels of commerce." The defendants refute this claim by placing handguns under a different legal heading—"unavoidably unsafe" products, which, by the current limits of technology, cannot be made completely safe for their intended use but are beneficial and so exempt from absolute liability.

From the premise of these arguments certain troubling questions naturally arise. For example, if strict product liability can be extended to lawful, properly functioning, but dangerous objects such as handguns, won't the makers of long guns, knives, axes, liquors, sleeping pills, cigarettes, and automobiles soon be made liable too, based on their products' potential to cause injury? After all, an automobile can be as deadly as a gun; as the cause of 55,000 deaths each year, cars easily best handguns as the leading cause of unnatural death. Should the courts decide whether a compact car is riskier than a large car, and place liability on its makers? Using the risk/utility test, Turley, Stein, and Corboy say that other products are potentially dangerous but causing injury is not their prime function, as it is the function of handguns; they all have other, beneficial uses that outweigh their occasional risks.

The use of product-liability law to instigate a sort of gun control is not a popular idea within the legal community. "I find myself in a very difficult position in this controversy," says Sheila Birnbaum, a product-liability specialist and professor of law at New York University Law School. "Though I believe in gun control, I think it should be accomplished by other means. My feeling is that tort law is being misused here. I am concerned that the tort system not be expanded to purposes for which it was not intended, to the point where the system might collapse." Even the professional organization of the plaintiff's bar, the American Trial Lawyers Association (ATLA), is shying away from any association with this kind of suit, to the disappointment of Windle Turley, who hoped it would take a strong stand of support.

Product-liability law has come under attack in the past few years as an unfair burden on the business community, a hindrance to industrial expansion and innovation, and an economic menace perpetrated by radical judges and ambulance-chasing lawyers. Although the basis for product liability is derived from ancient common law, it has undergone tremendous development and change in the past thirty years, with courts both widening the scope of corporate liability and easing the consumer's burden of proof. The increased popularity of such suits, and celebrated monetary awards made by juries (often later reduced by the judge), are precipitating a strong backlash. The legislatures of more than twenty states are considering or have passed product-liability "reform" bills, setting statutes of limitation, monetary-award ceilings, and other restrictions. Congress is considering a similar reform bill. Faced with this kind of public sentiment, the ATLA appears unwilling to lend support to a legal tactic that might further damage the reputation of product-liability law.

Another, larger, topic of concern is whether the courts should be handling gun-control decisions at all. Are courts the proper forum for arbitrating the merits of gun control, or should this public-policy decision be made only by the nation's elected representatives? To some, this is just another instance of the courts' meddling in policy and political issues, as they did in busing and abortion—trampling on the balance of power, ruling by judicial fiat.

It is the duty of the courts to make the law responsive to change and to rescue the public from the legislature's failure of nerve, say the litigation's supporters. But the legislatures have not failed, they have acted, the defendants reply: there are hundreds of federal, state, and local ordinances governing the possession of handguns. Congress and the states have never passed a strong, comprehensive gun-control measure because they have good reason not to: the American people don't want it. Look at the defeat of the California ballot initiative last November, they say. The inaction of the legislatures is a choice that the courts must not impinge upon. "If there is a proper sociological basis for gun control, lawmakers should pass a law," says David Maclay, legal counsel for Sturm Ruger & Co., Inc., a large handgun-manufacturing company. "They have not. That is proof to me that there isn't the proper sociological basis." Gun-control advocates view the legislatures as bodies that have sold their souls to the gun lobbyists, and look to the courtroom as a sanctuary of reason, where judges and juries cannot be so easily influenced.

The National Rifle Association is uncharacteristically keeping to the sidelines in this stage of the legal proceedings, although it naturally has strong opinions on the matter, and is watching developments closely. Michael McCabe, the association's general counsel, says, "It is inconceivable to me that a case could be won and upheld on appeal—the courts wouldn't sanction the legal theory or have the temerity to interfere with the prerogative of the legislature." But NRA lawyers are in consultation with the defense attorneys, and should any of the cases reach the appeal stage, the NRA will probably file an *amicus curiae* brief.

It would certainly be in the interests of the manufacturers for the NRA to dismiss the cases as a preposterous scare, because keeping calm will help keep the gunmakers' insurance rates from soaring. Spiraling insurance costs are a key element of the gun-control-by-litigation strategy. They are the mightiest club that can be held over the heads of the handgun industry—not a banning, not a restraining order, just enormous and continuous financial risk. If the courts place responsibility on the manufacturers to pay for damages, insurance companies will have to reevaluate policies completely and raise premiums, according to James Coonan, of Joseph Chiarello & Co., Inc., a brokerage house in New York that handles the insurance needs of more than twenty medium-sized gun manufacturers, including several being taken to court in the new lawsuits. "The exposure to risk is so farfetched," says Coonan, "that a rating approach is almost impossible." The insurers will no doubt think of something— probably putting the manufacturers into a special ultra-high-risk liability pool. It is the hope of Speiser and Turley that the insurance companies will put pressure on the gunmakers either to curtail their marketing of handguns severely, and so shield themselves from potential liability exposure, or to stop making the Saturday Night Special variety of handgun completely, for their own financial good.

The economic realm of this strategy is almost as complicated as the legal one. First, in the case of lawsuits against European manufacturers, there are the myriad difficulties of pursuing litigation against a foreign corporation, and then, if the plaintiffs win, the rigmarole of collecting damages through foreign insurers. As for lawsuits against domestic manufacturers, although there are a dozen or so large gunmakers (including Smith & Wesson, Colt, Sturm Ruger, and Charter Arms), much of the rest of the industry is composed of small shops in plants not much bigger than overgrown garages. Faced with the kinds of risks promised by these lawsuits, they will either go without insurance or go bankrupt. While gun-control activists might applaud their demise, others fear the loss of jobs and tax revenues.

There is always the possibility that gunmakers will weigh their potential liability losses against the size and elasticity of their market, and decide that it is still worth selling Saturday Night Specials to a clientele willing to pay an increased price. As it is, handgun prices are sure to rise, to absorb the legal fees the current lawsuits are costing the manufacturers. One gun-company president, David Ecker, of Charter Arms, in Stratford, Connecticut (defendant in one of Turley's suits), believes that the whole idea of making handguns so expensive that they can no longer be purchased freely by everyone is downright discrimination against the poor.

But the current lawsuits have a long road ahead before they seriously threaten the future of handgun manufacturers. The defendants in each case are asking the court to dismiss the suits against them, and though no judge has yet thrown out one of the important test cases, even Turley expects that some will be dismissed on points of law. Matters of fact might not be accepted by a jury, which could return a verdict of "no cause of action" against the manufacturers. Turley intends to have to endure several losses, but he is confident that his use of product-liability law will eventually prevail.

Should the plaintiffs win in a jury trial, the defendants will certainly appeal to a higher state court. The Brady case is to be tried in the federal district court for Washington, D.C., and the appeal would go to a panel of judges on the U.S. Court of Appeals. Their decision would become a federal precedent, which, while not binding on the state courts, would provide a strong influence. Though the cases will certainly be carried to the state supreme courts, none is likely to be heard before the U.S. Supreme Court, according to legal experts. As complicated as the cases are, they do not hinge on esoteric points of law that need definitive interpretation. In years past, the Supreme Court has refused to consider almost every product-liability case brought to it, and will probably do so again.

If the prevailing decisions of the courts turn out to be favorable to the plaintiffs, the gun suppliers might try to obtain a legislative remedy for their problems, asking for a special bill that would remove liability from their shoulders. Lobbyists for the gun industry might well ask their representatives to introduce such legislation. New bills might be modeled on the product-liability reform bills circulating now at the state and federal levels, or even be attached to them, but legal observers agree that they would be more effective on the state than on the national level. Even then, they would be difficult bills to draft if the courts of that state or any other had already placed liability on gunmakers; and any bill, even if it were successfully drafted and passed, could be challenged and brought back into court.

Stein's and Corboy's cases are still in their preliminary stages and at least a year away from trial. The first of Turley's cases should come to trial by the end of this year. It will be some time before the greatest hopes of the plaintiffs or the worst fears of the defendants can be realized; in the meantime, the deadly use of handguns will continue.

COME ARMED[2]

When Florida was looking for a slogan to attract tourists this year, it hit upon "Florida: the rules are different here". They are. Since October 1st a new law has made it easier in Florida than in any other large state in America to own and carry a pistol.

It is now legal for anyone except convicted felons, certified psychotics and twice-convicted drunks to carry handguns. The change in the law was designed to make it easier to carry a concealed weapon, but a loophole inadvertently made it legal to carry guns openly too. Better, you might think, to know that the man coming towards you is armed than to learn too late. Not in the eyes of Florida's legislators. They scrambled into an emergency session this week to make sure that guns stay out of sight.

In all but three counties in south-eastern Florida a gun can be bought on the spot, without a cooling-off period intended to keep someone from buying and using a gun in moments of passion. For $125, and after a few hours of firearms training, a buyer may obtain a permit that allows him to carry the weapon concealed on his person. Permits used to be available only to people who could

[2]Reprint of staffwritten article. Reprinted by permission from *The Economist*, O. 10, '87, p. 31. Copyright © 1987 by *The Economist*.

show the authorities that they had a good reason to be armed in public. Anyone who wants to carry a pistol may now do so.

The law's supporters say that criminals will now think twice before attacking someone. A well armed populace, they also argue, may put an end to massacres by mad gunmen. "Back in the old days," says the manager of the Tamiami Gun Shop, near Miami, "you never heard of mass killings because everybody was armed." That shop, like others, is now doing record business. By October 1st nearly 20,000 people around Miami and Fort Lauderdale had applied for permits to carry concealed guns, and as many have done so since.

The level of violence in Florida is already high. Last year 532 people died from gunshot wounds. In greater Miami alone, which had the state's toughest gun law until the new state law superseded it, 169 people were killed with handguns in 1986: more than died that way, in the same period, throughout Western Europe. But the law's supporters cite figures showing the rate of violent crime to be much higher in states where concealed weapons are illegal than in those where they are legal.

For the National Rifle Association, the new law is the triumphant culmination of a three-year battle against those local governments that impose restrictions on handguns. Instead of trying to rescind such laws town by town, the NRA took its case to a higher authority, the state legislature. This has long been dominated by rural conservatives, who were joined on the gun-law issue by Cuban legislators from Miami; many Cuban exiles view private gun ownership as a deterrent to communist takeovers. The law passed both houses of the legislature with more than two-thirds votes.

A LETHAL LUCKY CHARM[3]

Clive Shepherd, a Miami firearms instructor, calls it "the talisman syndrome"—the feeling of security that he says some of his

[3]Reprint of an article by Mary McIver, *Maclean's* staffwriter. Reprinted by permission from *Maclean's*, Vol. 100 (O. 12, '87), pp. 59–60. Copyright © 1987 by *Maclean's*.

students experience when they carry a concealed weapon. The students, said Shepherd, regard a gun as a good-luck charm—similar to the bags of charmed bones that primitive people wear around their necks to ward off evil. But whether the desire to carry a gun results from superstition, fear or frustration, it appears to be firmly entrenched in the state of Florida, which, effective last week, now has among the most liberal gun laws in the United States.

In May, responding to widespread public demand and political pressure, the state government passed a bill that would allow anyone 21 and over who takes a firearms safety course and does not have a criminal record or a history of drug or alcohol abuse to purchase a $164 concealed-weapons permit. The bill, scheduled to become law on Oct. 1, has alarmed many Florida residents and angered antigun lobbyists. "We have temporarily run into a brick wall," declared Michael Beard, executive director of the Washington-based National Coalition to Ban Handguns. Still, some members of the police maintain that the law will not provoke aggressive behavior on the part of ordinary citizens. Said Cmdr. William Johnson of the Miami area Metro Dade Country Police Department: "Virtually anyone who wants to carry a gun already has one in his car, home or place of business perfectly legally. The only difference is that some people will be carrying them under their sports jackets as well."

The new legislation resulted from growing public outrage over violent crime in Florida. Only three other states—Texas, Nevada and Louisiana—have higher murder rates. Indeed, the city of Miami has the highest murder rate in the country at 32.9 per 100,000 people. "The streets are littered with victims," declared Florida state representative Ron Johnson during the debate on the concealed-weapons bill last spring. "We need to send a strong message to criminals that the next time you try to rape or kill someone, they may well be armed."

In marked contrast to Florida, jurisdictions that already have some of the toughest gun laws in the world are attempting to tighten controls even further. On. Sept. 22 the British government announced a ban on semiautomatic weapons following an Aug. 23 incident in the town of Hungerford, 100 km west of London, where Michael Ryan murdered 16 people with an AK-47 assault rifle. And in Canada, where the Criminal Code severely restricts the possession and use of firearms, Toronto police Insp.

Robert Crampton released a study documenting a steady rise in firearm-related offences. Declared the 51-year-old police veteran, who is seeking more restrictive gun laws: "What I would like to know is why the people of Canada feel a need to have a handgun, a rifle or a shotgun."

But in Florida an increasing number of officers say they feel that they cannot protect citizens adequately. When members of the Miami-based National Association of Chiefs of Police were asked in a survey this year if they thought that their inability to protect the public was reason enough for an armed citizenry, more than 80 per cent said yes. Said Gerald Arenberg, the association's executive director: "You are more likely to find a policeman when you run a red light than when you need him in a violent situation."

Still, as the newly relaxed gun law was about to go into effect, state and local police prepared to meet potential dangers. In Fort Lauderdale, police chief Joseph Gerwens ordered his men to stop anyone they see carrying a weapon and disarm them until their right to carry the weapon is checked out. Asked if such actions might be regarded as harassment, Gerwens conceded, "I'm not sure how legal that all is."

Meanwhile, owners of Florida gun shops licensed to give instruction said that large numbers of prospective applicants have been signing up for the firearms safety courses—which can be completed in as little as an hour and do not necessarily require the students to fire a single shot. Some of the larger stores reported that their training centres are "graduating" as many as 200 people a week. Owners say that many of the applicants already owned handguns and took the course merely to gain permission to carry them.

But instructor Shepherd said that he anticipates a rise in new weapons sales—and he said that he is concerned about the minimal instruction requirements for their use. He predicted that some people will shoot themselves and that others will panic when confronted with a potentially lethal situation. "There are psychological and moral considerations that have to be dealt with," Shepherd declared. "Not everyone can pull the trigger." But as far as antihandgun activists are concerned, too many Florida citizens are eager to do just that.

EVEN THE NRA CAN HAVE A BAD DAY[4]

It looked like the blueprint for a typical National Rifle Association lobbying drive: Shower legislators with telegrams seeking support on a firearms bill. Get endorsements from prominent police and political leaders. Urge members to phone lawmakers and buttonhole them in hallways. It happened like clockwork last week in Maryland's State House. But this time, it was the NRA's enemies who used the formula to win a new form of gun control that may spread to other states: Empowering a government panel to ban the cheap handguns often used in street crimes and family squabbles.

The drive started with an NRA move to void a 1985 court decision that held gun makers potentially liable for deaths or injuries their weapons cause. The NRA won early rounds in a state that usually has bowed to its wishes. But the plan backfired when opponents mobilized behind an alternative bill aimed at "Saturday-night specials," which account for 1 in 5 seized firearms. They peppered legislators with messages from Martin Luther King's widow Coretta, and Sarah Brady, wife of James Brady, the White House press secretary wounded in fire from a cheap pistol in 1981. Police leaders, who split with the NRA on gun control a few years ago, were enlisted in the cause. "We mimicked NRA lobbying tactics," says Peter Franchot, a Maryland legislator.

Gun foes hope to capitalize. "We've slowed the NRA," claimed Michael Beard of the National Coalition to Ban Handguns. An early target: New Jersey, where State Senate President John Russo wants all handguns banned.

The NRA won't play dead. Last week, it helped persuade Vermont to become the 34th state to bar localities from curbing guns. The group also is winning support for laws similar to a new Florida measure making it easier to carry concealed guns in self-defense. "We need more mandatory prison terms for criminals, not handgun bans," says the NRA's Ted Lattanzio. "Gun opponents are resorting to emotional hysteria."

---

[4]Reprint of a staffwritten article. Reprinted by permission from *U.S. News & World Report*, Ap. 25, '88, p. 15. Copyright © 1988 by *U.S. News & World Report*.

Hysteria or no, antigun forces will use the Maryland triumph to put the NRA in a defensive stance. "The NRA lost in a state where it cut its political teeth in the '70s and has bragged about it ever since," says an antigun strategist, who vowed to "take the new law around the U.S. to show that the NRA can be a paper tiger."

BIBLIOGRAPHY

An asterisk (*) preceding a reference indicates that the article or part of it has been reprinted in this book.

BOOKS AND PAMPHLETS

Anderson, Jervis. Guns in American life. Random House. '84.

*Anon. Handgun control. Handgun Control, Inc.

*Anon. Handgun facts: twelve questions and answers about handgun control. Handgun Control, Inc.

*Anon. A question of self-defense. National Rifle Association.

*Anon. Ten myths about gun control. National Rifle Association.

Casey, Verna. Gun control; a selected bibliography. Vance. '88.

Cook, Phillip J. and Lambert, D., eds. Gun control. American Academy of Political and Social Science. '81.

Draper, Thomas, ed. The issue of gun control. H. W. Wilson. '81.

Foster, Carol D., et al. Gun control: restricting rights or protecting people? Information Aids. '87.

Gottlieb, Alan M. The rights of gun owners: a second amendment foundation handbook. Gordon Press. '86.

Halbrook, Stephen P. That every man be armed: the evolution of a constitutional right. University of New Mexico Press. '84.

Hardy, David T. Origins and development of the second amendment. Blacksmith Corporation. '86.

Kates, Don B., Jr., ed. Firearms and violence: issues of public policy. Pacific Institute for Public Policy Research. '84.

Kruscheke, Earl R. The right to keep and bear arms: a continuing American dilemma. Charles C. Thomas. '85.

Leddy, Edward E. Magnum force lobby: the National Rifle Association fights gun control. University Press of America. '87.

Lester, David. Gun control: issues and answers. Charles C. Thomas. '84.

Shields, Pete. Guns don't die—people do. Arbor House. '81.

Stewart, Alva W. Gun control: its pros & cons: a checklist. Vance. '86.

Wright, James D. Weapons, crime, and violence in America: a literature review and research agenda. U. S. Department of Justice. '81.

Wright, James D. Armed and considered dangerous: a survey of felons and their firearms. Aldine de Gruyter. '86.

Wright, James D., Rossi, Peter H., and Daly, Kathleen. Under the gun: weapons, crime and violence in America. Aldine de Gruyter. '83.

Zimring, Franklin E. and Hawkins, Gordon. The citizen's guide to gun control. Macmillan. '87.

Periodicals

*Shooting down gun myths. Spitzer, Robert J. America. 152:468–69. Je. 8, '85.

What's new: "Saturday night special" sellers and makers are liable. American Bar Association Journal. 71:98. D. '85.

To keep and bear arms. American Rifleman. 133:40–43. S. '85.

Chicago police officials call city gun law a failure. American Rifleman. 133:51. S. '85.

Assault on semi-autos. American Rifleman. 135:44–47. Ap. '87.

*Guns in the courts. Weiss, Elaine F. Atlantic. 251:8–16. My. '83.

The gun controversy; to have or have not. Boston Magazine. 77:229–33. S. '85.

The NRA shoots itself in the foot. Gleckman, Howard and Harbrecht, Sandra D. Business Week. p. 44+. My. 16, '88.

U. S. gunmakers: the casualties pile up. King, Resa W. Business Week. p. 74+. My. 19, '86.

Explosive issue awaits U. S. House: gun-law revision. Curtis, J. Sitomer. Christian Science Monitor. p. 3. Ap. 7, '86.

Criminal dichotomies. Commonweal. 112:131–32. Mr. 8, '85.

*Should Congress adopt proposed relaxation of handgun controls? Stevens, Ted; Kennedy, Edward; Dole, Robert; McClure, James; Mathias, Charles; Matsunaga, Spark; Hatch, Orrin; Levin, Carl; Dodd, Christopher; Kasten, Robert; Kerry, John; Symms, Steven. Congressional Digest. 65:138–59. My. '86.

IACP fighting NRA attempt to repeal machine gun laws. Crime Control Digest. 20:39. S. 29, '86.

President signs legislation easing federal firearms control. Criminal Law Reporter: 39:2183–84. Je. 4, '86.

*Come armed. Economist. p. 31. O. 10, '87.

The case for guns. Elliott, Chip. Esquire. 99:416–25. Je. '83.

The burden of bearing arms. Smith, Adam. Esquire. 106:55–56. Jl. '86.

The National Rifle Association. Mann, E. B. Field & Stream. 88:52. S. '83.

Good intentions, lousy laws. Field & Stream. 90:37–39. F. '86.

Handguns must be kept away from the John Hinckleys of the world. Glamour. 84:96+. My. '86.

Guess who is the new marketing target for guns? You are. Glamour. 84:94. S. '86.

*The ideological origins of the second amendment. Shalhope, Robert E. Journal of American History. 69:599-614. D. '82.

*An armed community: the origins and meaning of the right to bear arms. Cress, Lawrence Delbert. Journal of American History. 71:22-42. Je. '84.

*The second amendment and the right to bear arms: an exchange. Shalhope, Robert E. and Cress, Lawrence Delbert. Journal of American History. 71:587-93. D. '84.

The use of firearms in violent crime. Journal of Crime and Justice. 8:115-20. '85.

Rallying 'round the gun-control issue: police groups unite to battle McClure-Volkmer bill. Law Enforcement News. 11:1, 7. F. 24, '86.

Police groups try to cut NRA off at the pass. Nislow, Jennifer. Law Enforcement News. 11:1, 12. Mr. 24, '86.

Machine gun sales soaring. Law Enforcement News. 12:3. Je. 23, '86.

Reagan signs S. 49 gun bill as NRA eyes repeal of ban on machine guns. Law Enforcement News. 12:1, 5. Jl. 9, '86.

Eased gun control is pressed despite strong opposition. Los Angeles Times. Sect. I, p. 1. Ap. 9, '86.

Law, order, and gun control. Los Angeles Times. Sect. II, p. 4. Ap. 9, '86.

*A lethal lucky charm. McIver, Mary. Maclean's. 100:59-60. O. 12, '87.

You can get a girl with a gun. Harrison, Barbara Gruzzutti. Mademoiselle. 91:148. Jl. '85.

Out of sight, out of luck. Woods, Bruce. Mother Earth News. 107:96-98. S./O. '87.

Drop those guns. Nation. 239:573. D. 1, '84.

Subways are for shooting. Nation. 244:871. Je. 27, '87.

A verdict by their peers. Blecker, Robert. Nation. 245:334-36. O. 3, '87.

Guns of February. Kopkind, Andrew. Nation. 246:184-85. F. 13, '88.

Is government on the side of the thugs? National Review. 38:20. F. 14, '86.

Goetz, at last. National Review. 39:18-20. F. 13, '87.

Goetz and the future of New York. National Review. 39:19. Jl. 17, '87.

The Goetz confession. Mano, D. Keith. National Review. 40:60-62. My. 13, '88.

Crime/s ammunition. New Republic. 188:8. Mr. 7, '83.

*Gaga over guns. New Republic. 188:9-10. My. 30, '83.

*Under the gun. New Republic. 193:7-8. Ag. 26, '85.

Shots in the basement. Weisberg, Jacob. New Republic. 194:12-13. Ap. 14, '86.

Sons of guns. Saletan, William. New Republic. 196:11–13. Mr. 2, '87.

Whatever Bernie wants. New Republic. 197:9–10. Jl. 13/20, '87.

Go ahead, make our day. New Republic. 198:7–9. F. 22, '88.

House in middle as police and rifle group fight over legislation. New York Times. p. A23. Mr. 20, '86.

Goetz on trial. Fletcher, George P. New York Review of Books. 34:22–24+. Ap. 23, '87.

Florida bills to ease curbs on concealed firearms. New York Times. p. 14. My. 13, '87.

*An extraordinary people. Anderson, Jervis. New Yorker. 60:109–28+. N. 12, '84.

Notes from the underground. Logan, Andy. New Yorker. 60:72–76+. Ja. 28, '85.

An NRA shoot-out in Phoenix. Shapiro, Walter. Newsweek. 101:36. My. 16, '83.

A town on the edge of fear. Strasser, Steven. Newsweek. 103:27. Ja. 23, '84.

A Goetz backlash. Morganthau, Tom. Newsweek. 105:50–51+. Mr. 11, '85.

*Machine gun U.S.A. Morganthau, Tom. Newsweek. 106:46–50+. O. 14, '85.

Sarah Brady's crusade. Miller, Mark. Newsweek. 107:22. Ap. 14, '86.

Bernie Goetz goes on trial. Morganthau, Tom. Newsweek. 109:30. My. 11, '87.

*Battle over the plastic gun. Hackett, George. Newsweek. 109:31. Je. 1, '87.

Wyatt Earp comes to the sunshine state. Newsweek. 110:42. O. 12, '87.

*Kids: deadly force. Hackett, George. Newsweek. 111:18–19. Ja. 11, '88.

The handgun banners' next ploy. Starnes, Richard. Outdoor Life (Northeast edition). 171:54+. Mr. '83.

Should hunters pay for crime? Williamson, Lonnie. Outdoor Life (Northeast edition). 172:14+. Jl. '83.

A good gun law. Williamson, Lonnie. Outdoor Life. 177:34+. Mr. '86.

McClure/Volkmer: this bill endangers police. Police Chief. 53:24–25. Ja. '86.

*Wretchedness is a warm gun. Lueders, Bill. Progressive. 48:50. N. '84.

Guns: homewreckers or protectors? Hall, Holly. Psychology Today. 20:15. S. '86.

California sticks to its guns. Epstein, Fred. Rolling Stone. 19–21+. F. 17, '83.

Aiming to please. Epstein, Fred. Rolling Stone. 61–62. O. 13, '83.

Vigilantism. Dorfman, Andrea. Science Digest. 93:38–39. Jl. '85.

Homeguard. Scientific American. 255:68. S. '86.

Plastic guns are easy to smuggle through detectors, Rep. Biaggi tells subcommittee. Security Systems Digest. 17:3–4. My. 26, '86.

Up in arms over crime. Magnuson, Ed. Time. 125:28–31+. Ap. 8, '85.

Weapon of choice. Stengel, Richard. Time. 126:42–43. S. 9, '85.

Houston gun play. Time. 127:46. Mr. 10, '86.

*Defeat for a thin blue line. Doerner, William R. Time. 127:32. Ap. 21, '86.

Not guilty. Friedrich, Otto. Time. 129:10–11. Je. 29, '87.

Pistol packers. Garcia, Christina. Time. 130:28. S. 28, '87.

When women take up arms. Gibbs, Nancy R. Time. 131:63. Ap. 11, '88.

Gunning for it. Time. 131:58. Je. 27, '88.

Handguns are an occasion of sin. Mack, Michael. U. S. Catholic. 53:15–20. Mr. '88.

Fed-up shopkeepers strap on their guns. Galloway, Joseph L. U. S. News & World Report. 95:30–31. Ag. 22, '83.

Grass-roots war over gun control. U. S. News & World Report. 95:17. O. 17, '83.

High noon on gun control. Evans, Harold. U. S. News & World Report. 100:74. Mr. 17, '86.

Congress in a cross fire in a battle over gun control. Gest, Ted. U. S. News & World Report. 100:20–21. Mr. 24, '86.

Congress makes the NRA's day. Gest, Ted. U.S. News & World Report. 100:8. Ap. 21, '86.

*Dissidents, old allies shake NRA. Gest, Ted. U. S. News & World Report. 102:44. Ap. 27, '87.

Local gun controls bite the dust. Gest, Ted. U. S. News & World Report. 102:14–15. My. 25, '87.

Florida's new crop of pistol packers. Gest, Ted. U. S. News & World Report. 103:16. O. 12, '87.

*Even the NRA can have a bad day. U. S. News & World Report. 104:15. Ap. 25, '88.

Arming citizens to fight crime. Borzelieri, Frank. USA Today (magazine). 114:56–57. Jl. '85.

The rhetoric of the NRA. Rodgers, Raymond S. Vital Speeches of the Day. 49:758–61. O. 1, '83.

Liberals: the NRA's best friends. Gould, Leslie, Jr. Washington Monthly. 15:36–41. Ap. '83.

The NRA is right. Sugarman, Josh. Washington Monthly. 19:11–15. Je. '87.

The NRA's new killer instinct. Washington Post. p. A24. S. 24, '87.

Why police want gun laws. Editorial. Washington Post. p. A10. F. 22, '88.